NEEDLEPOINT
A Foundation Course

NEEDLEPOINT
A Foundation Course

Sandra Hardy

Guild of Master Craftsman Publications Ltd

First published 1998 by
Guild of Master Craftsman Publications Ltd,
166 High Street, Lewes,
East Sussex BN7 1XU

All photographs by Zul Mukhida

Needlepoint charts produced by Ethan Danielson

Line drawings by Ethan Danielson

ISBN 1 86108 082 4

Designed by Teresa Dearlove

Set in Sabon
Colour origination by Viscan Graphics (Singapore)
Printed and bound by Kyodo Printing (Singapore)
under the supervision of MRM Graphics,
Winslow, Buckinghamshire, UK

Measurements

Although care has been taken to ensure that the imperial measurements are accurate, they are only conversions from metric, and have been rounded up or down to the nearest quarter inch in most cases, or, in the case of very small measurements, the nearest one-eighth inch. Where large quantities of thread or yarn are called for in lists of materials, it should be understood that both metric and imperial quantities are only approximate. A conversion table is provided on page 135.

Canvas mesh sizes are given throughout in holes per inch (hpi), because this is still the unit of measurement used by manufacturers in English-speaking countries. European manufacturers normally measure them in holes per 10cm, and a conversion table for this appears on page 135.

Photocopying

Readers may find it useful to photocopy the needlepoint charts for their own use, so that they may be coloured in or enlarged (see page 7); but remember that all designs in this book are copyright and may not be reproduced commercially without the consent of the designer and copyright owner.

Contents

Acknowledgements	viii
List of Suppliers	viii
Preface	ix
Introduction	1

Part One   Basic Stitches

Continental Tent Stitch	10
1 Flower Needlecase	13
2 Flower and Fish Pincushion Chair Seat	15
Basketweave Stitch	20
3 Carnation Repeat-Patterned Glasses Case	22
Cross Stitch	25
4 William Morris-Style Pincushion	28
5 Rainbow Elephants Pencil Box Lid	31
Straight Stitch	34
6 Maple Leaf Cushion Panel	37

Part Two   Advanced Stitching Techniques

Crewel Wool Shading	44
7 Tropical Leaf Cushion Panel	46
Decorative Stitches	51
8 Picture Frame	54
9 Rug with Decorative Panels	57

Petit Point   63
10 Victorian Doll's House Carpet   65

Tramming   68
11 Georgian-Style Floral Seat Cover   70

Beadwork   74
12 Hearts and Flowers Sewing Box Lid   76

Waste Canvas   79
13 Animal Cushion   82

Part Three   Variation and Experimentation

Experimenting with Colour and Texture   88
14 Two Needlecases in Quilting Patterns   89
15 Space-Dyed Cushion   94

Designing Needlepoint   99
16 Spode Bellpull   108
17 Ship Drop-In Seat Cover   112
18 Strawberry and Cherry Tray   116

Making-Up Instructions   121

Metric/Imperial Conversion Tables   135
Index   136

Acknowledgements

The author would like to thank the following people and companies for supplying materials and items for displaying the needlepoint, and for help with stitching and making up the projects.

DMC for all the tapestry and crewel wools, soft and stranded cottons, seed beads, and all Zweigart canvases; and especially Cara Ackerman at DMC
Appletons for sample skeins of wool
Macleod Craft Marketing for the Caron threads
Colinette Yarns Ltd for the silk threads
Coats Crafts UK for Multi's embellishment yarn

Luxury Needlepoint for the wooden double pincushion (Project 4)
Stitchers: Ann Phillips, Jenny Hewer, Linda Williams, Pam Brown
Angela Secker for her expertise in making up the cushions
Also special thanks to my husband Norman for his word processing skills, and to my daughters Charlotte, Alicia and Gemma for charting, stitching and numerous other helpful tasks
Finally, Candy Tiles for giving permission to base a project on one of their designs.

List of Suppliers

Appleton Bros. Ltd, Thames Works, Church Street, Chiswick, London W4 2PE
Candy Tiles Ltd, Heathfield, Newton Abbot, Devon TQ12 6RF
Colinette Yarns Ltd, The Old Baptist Chapel, Watergate Street, Llanfair Caereinion, Powys, Mid Wales SY21 0RB
Coats Crafts UK, McMullen Road, Darlington, County Durham DL1 1YQ
Dehaviland Embroidery, Monomark House, 27 Old Gloucester Street, London WC1 3XX
DMC Creative World Ltd, Pullman Road, Wigston, Leics. LE18 2DY

Brass bellpull ends (Project 16): Shades at Mace and Nairn, 89 Crane Street, Salisbury, Wiltshire SP1 2PY
Pencil box (Project 5) and Sewing box (Project 12): Canopia, PO Box 420, Uxbridge, Middlesex UB8 2GW
Double pincushion (Project 4): Luxury Needlepoint, Rock Channel, Rye, East Sussex TN31 7HJ
Wooden tray (Project 18): Kernocraft Woodturning, Wheal Virgin House, Unit 5, Consols, St Ives, Cornwall TR26 2HW

Preface

Welcome to the wonderful world of needlepoint!

This book has been designed to start at the beginning, supplying you with all the basic information you need to get started. There are plenty of suggestions to help you get the best results, with explanations for 'using and doing' at all stages. Once the four basic stitches of tent, basketweave, cross, and straight are mastered, chapters move swiftly on to a variety of exciting advanced techniques: beadwork, tramming, crewel wool shading, and so on. To help you gain maximum benefit from the projects, there are ideas and suggestions for adapting and altering designs in order to suit everyone's taste and requirements.

The third section explores the rich diversity of available threads, and the use of dyeing methods to create your own original and stunning effects. The fascinating process of designing your own needlepoint is looked at step by step, with three projects based on commercial designs. Finally, clear instructions for making up the projects will ensure a truly professional finish to your beautiful needlepoint.

This book has been a delight both to design and to stitch, and I hope that you too will derive many hours of pleasure from it.

Sandra Hardy

Introduction

Needlepoint is embroidery worked on a base of canvas. It is sometimes referred to loosely as tapestry or canvas work, but, strictly speaking, tapestry is a woven rather than an embroidered fabric, while canvas work covers a number of other crafts involving canvas.

The basic skills and techniques of needlepoint are easily learnt. They rely, however, on the following prerequisites: selecting

- the correct size, type, and colour of canvas
- the right type and size of needle
- the appropriate thickness and fibre content of yarn, and
- the most suitable stitch for the purpose of the project.

Once these choices have been made you are well on your way to successful stitching. This Introduction looks at canvas, yarn, needles and threading, distortion of the canvas, and frames, while the four basic needlepoint stitches are investigated in the following chapters.

Canvas

Needlepoint is always worked on canvas, which is usually made of a stiffened cotton, but can be composed of silk, linen, or synthetic fibre. The canvas has a mesh of warp and weft threads, and it is the manner in which this is woven that distinguishes one type from another.

The three main varieties are:
- **mono** or **single**, where the warp and weft threads simply alternate in lying under and over one another;
- **interlock**, where two thinner vertical threads are twisted around a thicker horizontal one. This produces a more stable mesh than mono, and it is because of this that **blocking** or stretching a distorted canvas back to shape proves to be difficult;
- **double** or **Penelope**, made up of pairs of vertical and horizontal threads, providing a strong mesh. This has the added advantage of allowing the stitcher to use every hole for very fine stitching. It is sometimes labelled with two numbers instead of the usual one – e.g. 11/22, meaning 11 holes and 22 threads per inch.

Two specialist canvases available are **waste** canvas, which is a disposable one (see pages 79–81), and **plastic** canvas made from moulded plastic. This is ideal for children's and three-dimensional projects, and recently a smaller 14 gauge has been added to the larger 5, 7, and 10 hpi.

1

Canvas mesh sizes are still usually measured in holes per inch (hpi), even though the canvas is now supplied in metric sizes (1in = 2.5cm). (Manufacturers in continental Europe normally use holes per 10cm; a conversion table is provided on page 135.) Meshes vary from 3 to over 30 hpi, and it is this number by which canvas is selected. Rugs and large upholstery coverings would need the larger gauges, whilst fine work requires many more holes to the inch in order to achieve the desired detail. You will notice that a range of the most popular gauges has been used for the projects in this book, from 7 hpi for the rug to 22 hpi for the picture frame. The average sizes for cushions and small chair seats are between 11 and 14 hpi.

White, ecru, and antique are the most usual canvas colours, and it is best to use the white or ecru for light-coloured yarns, and the antique for darker colour schemes, as specks of canvas can sometimes show through. There is now a range of pastel shades of canvas in the smaller gauges, the yellow used for the Picture Frame (Project 8) being one of these. Using decorative stitches which do not fully cover the canvas is no longer a problem with these coloured backgrounds, whilst deliberately leaving areas unstitched can become a design feature. Widths of canvas vary from 48cm (18in) to 120cm (48in), with the rug canvases being the widest. As several widths are normally available in each size and type, choose the most economical width for the specific project.

Finally, the cost of canvas varies enormously, depending on the quality. The cheapest ones may have several irregularities and slubs in the weave, subsequently causing unevenness in the stitching. There is a polished de luxe version which is ideal for projects requiring strength and durability, such as chair coverings.

Yarn

Tapestry, crewel, and Persian wools are the most-used yarns for needlepoint. They consist of 100% pure wool and are colourfast, but less fluffy and soft than knitting wool. This is because they have been manufactured specifically to withstand abrasion, which occurs both in the stitching process and when the finished item is in use. Generally the wool is sold in skeins, with some

Suitable Yarns for Needlepoint

Brand name	Description	Whether divisible into strands	Number of shades	Length of skein	Length of hank
Appletons' Tapestry Wool	Twisted, smooth 4-ply yarn	Not advisable	420	10m	56m
Appletons' Crewel Wool	Soft and strong 2-ply yarn	Strands can be used singly or 2 or 3 together	420	25m	195m
Anchor (Coats Patons) Tapisserie	Twisted 3-ply strong yarn	Not advisable	475	10m	40m approx. (66 colours)
Paterna Persian	3-stranded loosely twisted 2-ply with a distinct nap – one direction smooth, the other rough	Easily separated into 3 strands	417	8m	Not available
DMC Tapestry Wool	Smooth, twisted 4-ply	Not advisable	463	8m	38m (80 colours)
DMC Broder Medicis	Fine, soft crewel wool	Not advisable	180	25m	480m approx.

manufacturers supplying hanks, which are ideal for larger projects. Rug wool is tougher and coarser, of 2, 4, 6, or 8-ply thickness, and often includes rayon, viscose, or cotton combined with the wool. The table on page 2 compares the main brands available in the UK.

The colour range of these wools is enormous, from the subdued and muted, right through to pretty pastel shades and deep rich tones, to almost fluorescent bright colours. New shades are being added constantly as demand requires, and it is interesting to note that Appletons' original colour range of 1946 still exists, but of course with numerous additions. This vast choice of colours makes it possible to select an authentic colour scheme for any historical period.

The ranges of stranded, perle, and soft cotton, as well as stranded silk, can be very successfully used for needlepoint projects. These would be suitable for decorative items rather than for those subject to wear and tear. A small sample would need to be stitched first, using the chosen canvas size and stitch, so that the appropriate number of strands of thread can be decided upon.

Needles

Needlepoint is worked with tapestry needles, which differ from most other types of needle in that they have a blunt tip rather than a pointed one. This is essential so that the canvas threads and the wool itself are not caught or split whilst stitching. The needles also have a large eye, which is necessary for the thickness of thread generally used. The range of sizes goes from 13 (the largest) to 26, and the correct size must be selected for the canvas gauge and yarn

thickness (see the table below). If too small a size is used the wool tends to twist, fray, and wear thin, while too large a needle will force the canvas mesh apart, leaving enlarged and distorted areas.

Choosing the Right Needle

Canvas mesh size (hpi)	Recommended needle size
3, 4, 5, 6	13 (largest available)
7, 8, 9	16
10, 11, 12	18
13, 14, 15	20
16, 17, 18, 20	22
22, 24	24
Finer than 24	26 (smallest available)

Threading the needle

Commercial needle-threaders of metal and wire can be very helpful, but often are only strong enough for the thinner needlepoint wools. Alternatively, try the paper strip or loop methods illustrated here.

Threading the needle: paper strip method.

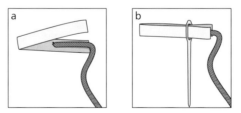

For the paper method, cut a strip of paper 5mm (³⁄₁₆in) wide and fold in half with the wool inside it. Push this through the eye of the needle.

Threading the needle: loop method.

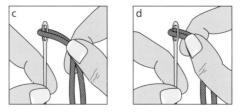

For the loop method, wrap the thread around the needle, holding it tightly. Slide the thread off the end of the needle and push it through the needle eye.

Distortion of the canvas

Depending mainly on the stitch used, and to a lesser extent on the type of yarn, canvas, and tension, distortion of the canvas can occur whilst stitching. The real culprit is the continental tent stitch, which if used on unframed canvas will transform an original square into a well-defined trapezium shape. Even the stitches recommended for not causing distortion, however, do often create a small amount of misshaping. This distortion must then be **blocked** or stretched back to shape. Many people find this not only a tiresome exercise, but often quite difficult. The easy solution is to use a frame whilst stitching; as long as the canvas is connected so that it is taut both vertically and horizontally, then 95% of any likely distortion will be eliminated.

There are several different types of frame available, all with their advantages and disadvantages. Sizes vary from 15 x 30cm (6 x 12in) up to a maximum width of 122cm (48in).

The **stretcher frame**, the simplest type, resembles a picture frame, and can easily be made up from two pairs of artist's stretchers, which come with corners mitred and slotted ready for assembly. It is important that the frame is large enough to take the whole extent of the canvas, so this type of frame would not be suitable for a very large project. The canvas is attached to the frame with drawing pins or staples.

Attaching canvas to a stretcher frame.

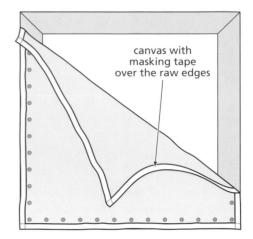

canvas with masking tape over the raw edges

Slate or **rotating frames** consist of two horizontal rollers with tape attached, and two side-bars. The canvas is stitched to the top and bottom tapes, and then laced down the sides over the side-bars. Again, it is essential that the frame is wide enough for the required canvas, but excess length can be wound round the horizontal rollers.

Attaching canvas to a slate or rotating frame.

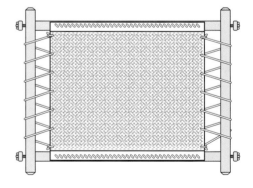

The larger **floor-standing frames**, and some smaller ones, with a **clamp** or **clip-on system**, leave both hands free for stitching. This speeds up the stitching process, as one hand can be positioned above the canvas and one below.

Tubular PVC frames are relatively recent, and simply clamp the canvas on all sides between the frame. However, the canvas tends to slacken with use, which makes constant retightening necessary.

If a very small piece of canvas is being worked, an embroidery hoop would be an ideal size of frame, except that the canvas is usually too thick and tensioning becomes impossible. A solution is to attach the small square of canvas to a strong, thin, fabric such as calico. Machine-stitch the canvas and calico together if possible, for speed and strength, and then place the whole in a larger embroidery hoop.

Using a frame has other advantages besides the main one of reducing distortion, but also has disadvantages. The decision whether to use one or not is a matter of personal preference.

Advantages

- The frame substantially reduces distortion.
- Under tension, puckering of the canvas is avoided, and a more even tension of stitching is produced.
- Handling of the canvas and stitched areas is reduced.
- It is easier to count the threads to position the designs when the canvas is held firmly.

Disadvantages

- Attaching the canvas to the frame takes some time. It should be fixed on all four sides for maximum effect.
- The needlepoint becomes less portable when attached to a frame, particularly if it is a large project.
- The size and design of the frame mean that often only one section of the work can be viewed at any time.

Now that the basic considerations have been dealt with, here are several sugges-tions which will further enhance your work, helping you to achieve a satis-fying, professional standard.

For best results

- Cut the hanks of wool into two equal pieces, which will give you ready-to-use lengths of approxi-mately 75cm (30in). For fine canvases of 14 hpi and above, cut hanks into three lengths to prevent tangling. Make similar lengths when cutting skeins.
- Whilst stitching, move the needle along the wool from time to time, or it will wear thin at the point where the needle is.
- At frequent intervals whilst stitching, let the needle and thread dangle freely to unwind any twists.
- Whenever possible, bring needle and yarn up into an **empty** hole – that is, one without any stitches already using it – and down into one already holding a stitch. This will cause least disturbance to the stitching and pull any loose fibres through to the wrong side.
- Discard any lengths of thread which seem particularly thick or thin, and of course any knots which sometimes occur.
- Never re-stitch any unpicked wool, as it will have become untwisted, stretched, and generally damaged.
- Try not to stop and leave work in the middle of a row, as the tension will gradually slacken.
- Try not to start a new length of thread in the middle of a row, as the new length will often appear slightly thicker.
- Start background stitching at the top of the canvas and work downwards,

so that the stitched work is not being constantly rubbed.

- When using very light colours, try to stitch these last so that the work does not become soiled.

- Do not jump across from one area of stitching to another of the same colour, leaving a large stitch on the reverse side. Not only can this spoil the tension by being pulled too tight or left too loose, but it can cause bulk and a build-up of threads on the underside of the canvas.

- Never leave any ends on the wrong side not fully finished off, as strands will become caught in subsequent stitching and may even be pulled through to the right side, causing discolourment.

- Try to buy sufficient yarn at one time to complete a project, as dye lots vary. Estimate quantities by stitching a square inch (2.5 x 2.5cm) on the chosen canvas size using the correct stitch, then multiplying this by the number of square inches in the complete project.

- When stitching is completed, hold the canvas to the light so that any missed stitches can easily be seen.

Other equipment

Anglepoise lamps, with or without magnifiers, can be floor- or table-standing, or can even be attached to some tapestry frames. These can significantly help in providing good light at all times, preventing eye strain. Daylight simulation bulbs are particularly valuable for maintaining 'true' colours for evening or poor winter-daylight stitching.

Various palettes or thread organizers are available, and may be useful in keeping all or some of the threads separated while stitching.

Sharp scissors are essential, both small embroidery ones for cutting threads and larger ones for cutting canvas.

Finally, comfortable seating is essential, in terms of both seat height and adequate back support, especially if long hours are spent in the same position. Some frames are height-adjustable, which can be a real advantage.

Preparation for stitching

- Cut the canvas to the required size along a straight thread, remembering to leave a 5cm (2in) allowance on all four sides, and as much as 7.5cm (3in) for large projects. The shape of the canvas should always be square or rectangular to begin with. If a curved shape were cut for a round stool, attaching to a frame would be impossible, and blocking or stretching would be equally difficult.

- Mark any lines or centre points on the canvas with a permanent pen. Test that the pen is fully waterproof before using it, or, when the canvas is dampened for blocking, ink could seep through into the stitching. Alternatively, mark the canvas with tacking stitches and tailor tacks.

- Bind all the raw edges of the canvas with masking tape. This is quick and easy, but if you prefer, bias binding or tape could be stitched on instead.

- If a frame is being used, then attach the canvas in the appropriate way for the type of frame.

Starting to stitch

- Start all lengths of yarn with a knot on the right side. This should be positioned approximately 2.5cm (1in) from where you intend to start stitching, and in the direction that the stitching will progress. Once the thread underneath is covered over with stitches, then the knot can be cut away.
- Finish off all lengths by running the thread under several stitches on the wrong side, and then snipping off the end.

Working from a chart

To avoid confusion and mistakes when reading charts, remember that one chart square represents one canvas thread; always count threads, not holes, when positioning stitches.

It is quite easy when working from a chart to lose your place and subsequently make a mistake. There are several ways to prevent this from happening. First, mark the canvas at 10-thread intervals with a permanent pen or needle and cotton, to correspond with the heavy black line which appears on all charts. Against this marked grid it will be easier to check your stitching position. Secondly, it can be helpful to colour in the squares on the chart as they are stitched. Using photocopies can save marking the actual book chart, and this would also give the opportunity for enlarging the size of the chart. Alternatively, a clear plastic sheet can be placed over the chart and secured with paperclips, and then markings made on

this. A weighted magnifier could also be the answer, keeping the exact position on the chart, at the same time as enlarging it.

Repair and care of needlepoint

It is quite likely that some mistakes will be made whilst stitching. If these are only a few wrong stitches, then unthread the needle and pull them out. It is better now to end off this length of thread, as it is likely to be stretched and damaged. Re-stitch with a new length of thread.

If, however, a large area of stitching is incorrect, then the stitches will have to be cut and removed carefully. It may be that in this process one or two of the canvas threads are snipped by mistake. To repair this, cut a square of canvas of the same gauge, a few strands larger than the affected area. Place this behind the cut thread and backstitch into position, lining up the threads and holes accurately. Use a sewing thread in a matching colour to the canvas. Now re-stitch in the appropriate stitch and colour.

The biggest enemy to any piece of needlepoint over the years is dust. As with all fabrics and threads, dust will not only discolour, but eventually rot the fibres. The best way to clean needlepoint, then, is to vacuum regularly to remove this dust. If a piece of stitching definitely needs more cleaning than this it can be dry-cleaned or washed; both have their drawbacks. The solvents in the dry-cleaning process may damage the fibres, whereas washing may shrink the wool, cause dyes to run into one another, and return the stitching back to its original distorted shape.

Part One
Basic Stitches

Continental Tent Stitch

This stitch has been used for needlepoint throughout its history, not only because of its versatility but also for its strength and durability. The Elizabethan period saw a great spread of tent-stitch canvas work, worked in wools and silks, including very large wall hangings, table carpets, bed valances, and seating cushions. Tent stitch remained a firm favourite right up to and into the 18th century. Here Florentine or Bargello was introduced and instantly claimed immense popularity, especially for larger items, mainly because of its comparative speed of execution. Again in the 19th century tent stitch suffered a rival, but this time it was cross stitch; the quantity of printed charts for cross stitch using the very popular Berlin wools was vast. Earlier this century all canvas work was very much out of favour, and it is really only since the 1950s and 1960s that there has been a resurgence. This renewed interest in all aspects of canvas work has brought a revival in the more decorative stitches, especially for their textural qualities. However, continental tent stitch will remain a firm favourite as an ideal stitch for all the pictorial designs.

Working continental tent stitch

It is usually worked over one canvas thread in horizontal rows across the canvas, from right to left and from the top of the canvas downwards.

Method 1

The simplest way of continuing is to finish off the thread at the end of the row and to re-start on the right-hand side again (Fig 1.1). Continuing in this way ensures that all new stitches are coming up into an empty canvas hole,

Fig 1.1 Tent stitch, method 1.

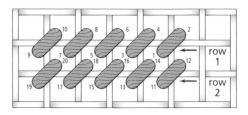

and going down into one already stitched. This will contribute greatly to the overall evenness of the stitching. However, the drawback of working this way is that if the rows are short there is a considerable amount of finishing and starting of threads.

Method 2

Alternatively, the first row can be stitched centrally in the area to be filled. Row 1 is worked as before from right to left; row 2 can now be stitched from left to right above row 1. Row 3 will be stitched below row 1 from right to left, and rows will continue to be stitched alternately above and below (Fig 1.2).

Fig 1.2 Tent stitch, method 2.

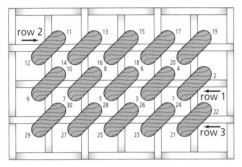

This method ensures that all stitches are emerging into empty canvas holes, but has the disadvantage that if the area to be stitched is of a fair size then long stitches from one row to the next will be present at the edges.

Some stitchers like to turn the canvas completely around after each row, so that they are always stitching in the same direction; this can contribute to overall evenness of the work.

Method 3

This gives continuous stitching from row to row in a downwards direction (Fig 1.3). However, all alternate rows

will be coming up into holes already stitched. This causes a disturbance of the yarn, which in turn can give an uneven tension. The overall effect is often one of 'ribbing', with alternate rows appearing larger and slacker.

Fig 1.3 Tent stitch, method 3.

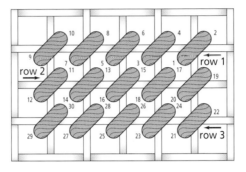

Continental tent stitch can be worked in single rows vertically if the design warrants it, or in a diagonal direction (Figs 1.4 and 1.5).

Fig 1.4 Tent stitch in vertical rows.

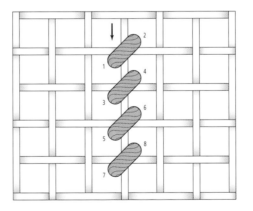

Fig 1.5 Tent stitch in diagonal rows.

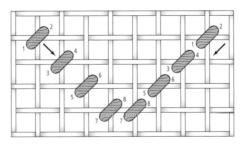

The inconsistency between left and right diagonal lines occurs with all diagonal stitches, such as basketweave and half-cross; this can sometimes spoil the effect of a design. If continuous lines are required, then two rows must be stitched instead of one. Alternatively, the same colour thread can be run underneath the line of stitches; however, this can create a slightly raised effect which could equally spoil the design. Of course, you could use a stitch which is the same in all directions, such as cross stitch.

Advantages

- It can be worked horizontally, vertically, and diagonally, making it very versatile.
- It is ideal for outlines, and creating curved shapes.
- It is just as suitable for small irregular areas as for large background ones.
- It covers the back of the canvas well, creating a padded surface for strength and durability.
- It is suitable for frequent colour changes in pictorial designs.

Disadvantages

- It distorts the canvas, because the stitches on both sides are pulling in the same direction.
- It uses more yarn than other similar-looking stitches.

1 Flower
Needlecase

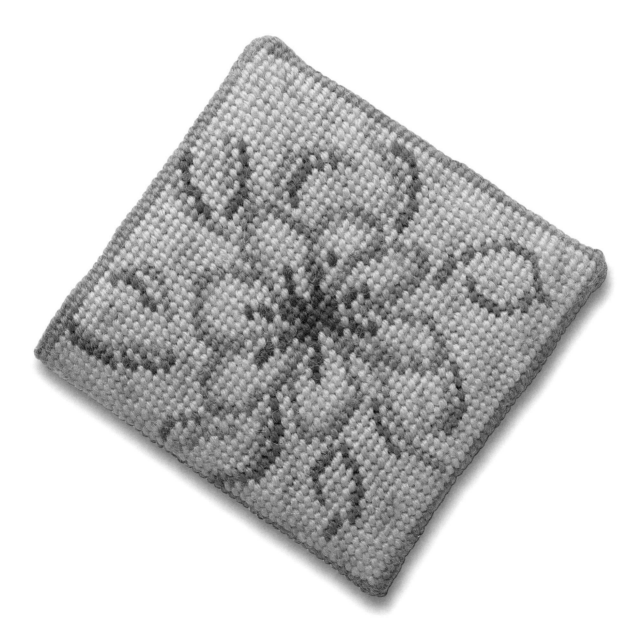

This bright, colourful design is a good starting project, and is stitched entirely in continental tent.

Finished size

10cm (4in) square

How to stitch the needlecase

1 Fold the canvas in half lengthways and mark this centre line from edge to edge. This will be stitched in blue 481 and acts as the dividing line between the two sides.

2 Count from the blue line on both sides to position and stitch the orange border. Remember to count the threads on the canvas, and that one hole on the chart represents one canvas thread.

3 For the flower side, stitch
- the petal outlines
- the yellow lines on the petals
- the petal background
- the green and blue lines
- the peach and blue shading on the

You will need

- 12 hpi interlock canvas, white, 15 x 25cm (6 x 10in)
- Appletons' tapestry wool:
  - 1 skein each of shades 421, 434, 481, 622, 623, 703, 871, 875, 996
  - 2 skeins 877
- tapestry needle, size 20
- 2oz (70g) polyester wadding,

background
- the background

4 For the second side, stitch
- the green and blue intersecting lines
- the orange petal outlines
- the dark orange middle and yellow shading
- the petal background
- the background shading in blue and peach
- the background.

5 To finish the needlecase, refer to the instructions on page 122.

- size 10 x 20cm (4 x 8in)
- piece of interlining, 10 x 20cm (4 x 8in)
- piece of matching lining fabric, 13 x 23cm (5 x 9in)
- piece of felt, 8 x 18cm (¾ x 7in)
- sewing thread to match the lining fabric

Key

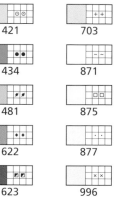

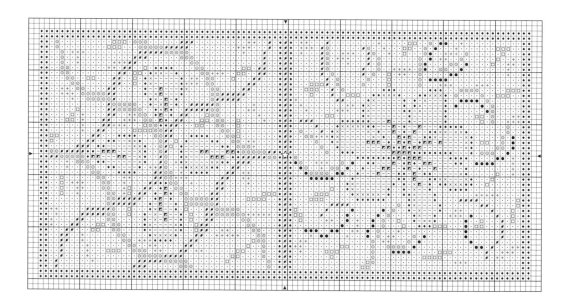

2 Flower and Fish Pincushion Chair Seat

This second project has used the earlier flower motif and patterns and has expanded and developed them into a modern full-size seat design. The green-and-blue patterned, friendly fishes contrast with the soft peachy background, while the sponged chair frame is reflected in the pale blue and darker peach mottled background. The co-ordinating braid uses the popular friendship bracelet technique, providing the final finishing touch. It is still a relatively easy project to stitch, and the irregular outlines, wavy and intersecting lines, and small patterns provide an ideal opportunity to master continental tent stitch fully.

The chair used for this project was actually a junk-shop find, and previously had a caned seat. Chairs of this type can easily be found, and are usually inexpensive. The broken cane was removed, the holes filled, the frame cleaned, painted, and sponged, and finally the seat space was upholstered.

Finished size

36 x 35cm (14 x 13in)

You will need

- 12 hpi white interlock canvas, 48cm (19in) square
- Appletons' tapestry wool:
  - 2½ hanks 877
  - ½ hank each of 421, 622
  - 2 skeins each of 434, 463, 481, 703, 871, 875, 996
  - 1 skein 623

- tapestry needle, size 20
- 2oz (70g) polyester wadding, 36 x 35cm (14 x 13½in)
- UHU glue
- 1.5m (5ft) braid

For the Braid
- 2 skeins each of 622, 703
- 1 skein 421

How to stitch the Seat Cover

1 Fold the canvas in half in both directions to find the centre point, and mark with a thread or permanent pen.

2 Attach to the frame in the usual way.

3 Use the centre mark to start stitching the central design in the following order:
- dark blue wavy lines
- fish outlines, patterns, background
- flower outline, middles, yellow or orange shading, background
- leaf lines around flowers
- blue and green intersecting lines, orange petal outlines, dark orange middles, yellow shading background
- orange and yellow squiggles (complete one colour then the other)
- background shading in pale blue and dark peach (only a small section has been charted, as these patches are totally random and irregular).

4 Finally fill in the pale peach background, stitching in as long rows as possible, from right to left starting at the top right side.

5 When complete, remove from the frame and check whether stretching is needed.

6 Instructions for stretching the panel, making the braid, and attaching the panel to the chair seat with the braid are given on pages 121 and 122–5.

For best results

- Where very small areas of one colour are to be stitched, do not jump over more than three threads to the next area, as this creates excess bulk, and can pull the canvas too tightly.
- Ensure that all the ends are neatly finished off on the wrong side, or these may be pulled through to the

right side with subsequent stitching.

- Try to minimize the number of darker threads on the back lying over unstitched background areas, as these tend to create dark shadows when the background stitching is in place.

Adapting this design

The size of this project will fit a standard pincushion chair seat; however, the measurements of your chair may not match exactly, so adjustments may have to be made. Extra can be easily added all round, by simply extending the background areas. To make the pattern smaller, there is approximately 2cm (¾in) of background in the width that can be removed without disturbing the main pattern. For the length, it is advisable to remove material from the top of the design only, so that the small fish at the bottom remains intact. You may like to stitch this design into a cushion, which can be easily done by squaring up the stitching, and adding a small border all the way around (see Fig 1.6). The final size of the cushion will be approximately a 41cm (16in) square.

Fig 1.6 Optional border design.

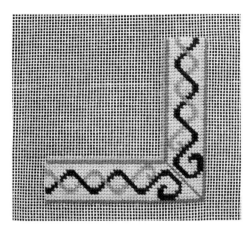

18

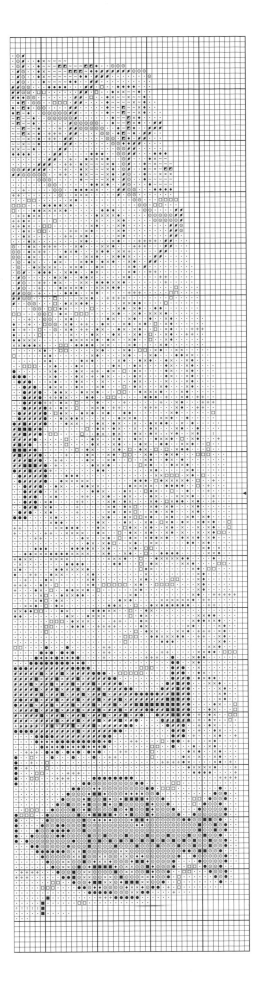

Key

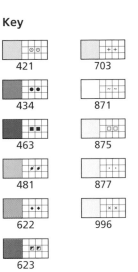

421

703

434

871

463

875

481

877

622

996

623

Basketweave Stitch

This is also known as diagonal tent stitch, because the right side is almost indistinguishable from that of continental tent. The difference, however, is easily seen on the wrong side, where the stitched threads resemble a basketweave pattern. During the Victorian period when Berlin woolwork was so popular, the name 'basketweave stitch' does not seem to have been in evidence, and yet the stitch itself was being worked. *The Illuminated Book of Needlework*, written in 1847 by Mrs Henry Owen, recommends that tent stitch for grounding (i.e. backgrounds) should also 'be worked on the cross', and the accompanying diagrams illustrate the basketweave-stitch method. Several projects in this book apart from the glasses case in this chapter, have used it for their backgrounds – such as the Rug and the Georgian Seat Cover (Projects 9 and 11).

Working basketweave stitch

It should be started in the top right-hand corner of the canvas and worked in diagonal rows across. Each row should alternate in its direction of working – first row up, second row down, third row up, etc. (see Fig 1.7). In all downward rows the needle is in a vertical position, and for all upward rows, a horizontal position.

Fig 1.7 Basketweave stitch.

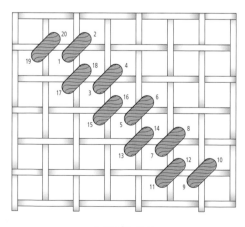

a Right side

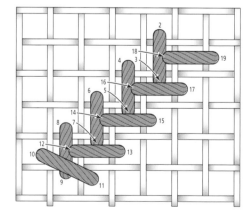

b Wrong side

Advantages

- Its main advantage, and the reason for its being used in preference to continental tent stitch, is that it does not distort the canvas, as the vertical and horizontal stitches on the back exert a counteracting pull.
- It is easy and relaxing to work once the basic method is mastered.
- It covers the canvas front well and creates a padded wrong side, making it very suitable for upholstered projects.

Disadvantages

- Faint ridges sometimes occur on the right side, spoiling the even appearance of the stitching. These are usually due to two rows together being stitched in the same direction, instead of alternately. It is a good idea to try to finish off a length of yarn not at the end of a row, but a short distance along the next; it is easy then to know in which direction the stitching should be continued. Care must be taken when stitching around a central motif that the sequence is maintained on both sides, until the rows meet up again. To finish off ends of threads, stitch back through the last few stitches completed, rather than in another direction, as this will help to achieve an even appearance on the right side.
- It is only suitable for large areas or blocks, and is quite impossible to use for the pictorial part of a design, where frequent colour changes and horizontal and vertical lines of stitching are required.

3 Carnation Repeat-Patterned Glasses Case

This design is a repeat pattern based on that much-loved flower, the carnation. Known in the 17th century as the 'gillyflower', it was second only in popularity to the rose. Throughout the centuries, its overall fan shape and attractive frilled edges have easily translated not only into needlepoint, but many other needlework techniques.

The simple pattern of this design has been enhanced not only by the two co-ordinating colours of the flowers, but by the randomly shaded background. The use of fine crewel wool has enabled the mixing of strands within the needle to achieve this subtly coloured effect. The handmade button adds the finishing touch to this item.

This is an ideal project for using wool or thread already bought, as the design could easily be stitched in a greater number of colours. It is also very suitable for changing in size by adding more flowers. In fact, repeat patterns such as this one make a very good project with which to start when designing your own needlepoint. Once the small design is decided on, it can be repeated endlessly to any size or shape.

Finished size

10 x 17cm (4 x 6¾in)

You will need

- 14 hpi canvas, white, 18 x 24cm (7 x 16½in)
- DMC Broder Medicis crewel wool:
  - 1 skein each of blanc, 8151, 8223, 8225, 8397, 8426, 8748, 8895, 8896, 8871
  - 5 skeins 8328
- tapestry needle, size 18
- 2oz (70g) polyester wadding, size 10 x 20cm (4 x 8in)
- lining fabric, 13 x 37cm (5½ x 14½in)
- small fabric-covered button
- approximately 8cm (3in) length of thin cord

How to stitch

1 Mark the centre line across the canvas widthways with a light-coloured permanent pen, and attach to a small frame.

2 Start stitching the uppermost flower first, in continental tent stitch, with three strands of wool, using the marked line for positioning.

3 From this, stitch the next flower in the diagonal line, then move on to the band of flowers below.

4 When the first three rows of flowers have been completed, turn the chart upside down and repeat for the second side.

5 Start stitching the background at the top right-hand corner, working diagonally across the canvas in basketweave stitch and around the flowers. Keep the wool colours fairly plain next to the flowers, so that there will be sufficient contrast, whilst in between, randomly mix the additional shades. Always keep at least one thread of the base colour (8328) in the needle for all stitching, to ensure consistency throughout.

6 Remove from the frame and sew right sides together following the instructions on page 125.

Key

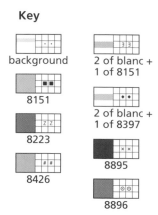

background

8151

8223

8426

2 of blanc +
1 of 8151

2 of blanc +
1 of 8397

8895

8896

Background colour consists
of at least one strand of
8328, mixed randomly with
strands of 8225, 8397,
8748, 8871 and blanc.

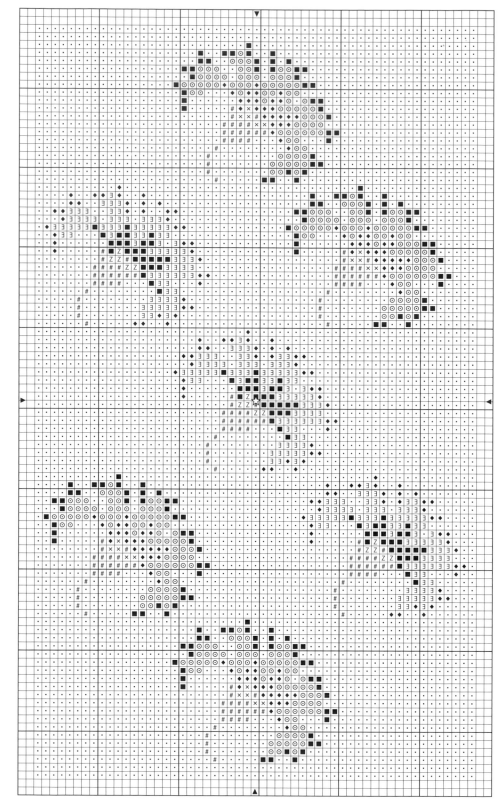

Cross Stitch

This is probably the oldest decorative stitch in the world, and has not only been used in many different types of embroidery, but by every ethnic group. However, it was in the Elizabethan period that cross stitch, along with tent stitch, became widespread, especially for domestic items. The famous Oxburgh hangings, part of which can be seen in the Victoria and Albert Museum, were stitched around 1570 in cross stitch of silk and gilt thread on a linen canvas by Mary, Queen of Scots and Bess of Hardwick. These consist of small medallions, such as 'A Great Munkey, Elephants, A Cherry Bush, A Boate Fish', etc., applied to a green velvet base forming four wall hangings. After this, tent stitch seems to have taken over in popularity, while cross stitch was confined to being used in conjunction with other stitches and as a means of highlighting. Its revival in the 19th century with the introduction of specially dyed Berlin wools and printed charts saw its use in every conceivable item from slippers to piano covers, purses to chair covers. The two main qualities of strength and durability, which attracted the Victorians to cross stitch, have meant that numerous pieces of canvas work, although faded in colour, are still in excellent condition

today. It is interesting to note that the trend today seems to be towards quicker to work stitches such as tent, basketweave, and straight stitch, with cross stitch confined to 'Victorian-style' kits. Through the years a number of related stitches have been developed; the simplest of these is half-cross, while composite varieties include Italian three-sided, double straight, and Montenegrin cross stitches (see Fig 1.8).

Fig 1.8 Varieties of cross stitch.

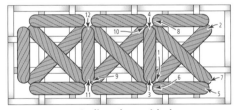

a Italian three-sided

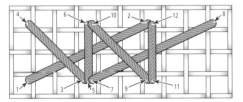

b Montenegrin

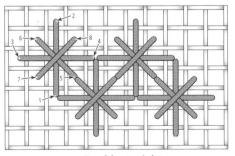

c Double straight

Working cross stitch

Each cross stitch consists of two diagonal stitches placed one over the other in the shape of a cross. Cross stitch is usually worked over one canvas thread in horizontal rows, but can be worked vertically or diagonally. Several methods exist, but all agree that the uppermost stitch of each 'cross' should lie in the same direction.

Method 1

Work single diagonal stitches from left to right along a row, and then return working from right to left crossing over all the stitches (Fig 1.9). This gives an even appearance to the stitching and uses the smallest amount of thread.

Fig 1.9 Cross stitch, method 1.

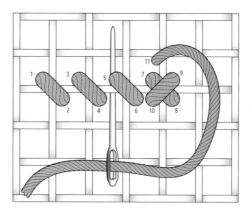

Method 2

Each cross is completed before proceeding to the next (Fig 1.10). This leaves more yarn on the reverse side, giving extra padding for added durability.

Fig 1.10 Cross stitch, method 2.

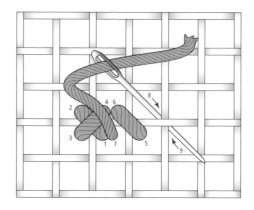

Method 3

A variation of the above method, again providing a well-padded reverse side (Fig 1.11).

Fig 1.11 Cross stitch, method 3.

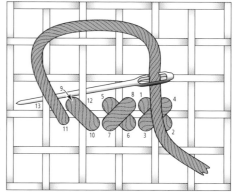

Advantages

- Each stitch creates a complete square, thus eliminating the design problems of one-directional stitches.
- A square needlepoint with minimal distortion is achieved, because there is an identical number of stitches in each direction.
- As a frame is not necessary, the stitching process can be made quicker by working some of the

stitch movements in one process – for example, by inserting the needle through the canvas and bringing it through to the front again in one movement, which cannot be done when the canvas is stretched taut on a frame.

- It is suitable for a wide range of items, as the thickness of the reverse side can be regulated by the stitching method.

Disadvantages

- If the canvas is framed – which will improve the evenness of the tension – the stitching will be more time-consuming than continental tent stitch or basketweave.
- Depending on the method of stitching selected, a large quantity of yarn may be used.

Half-cross stitch

This has been worked throughout history alongside cross stitch, although it has never been as popular for needlepoint. It does not always cover the front of the canvas well, and hardly covers the reverse side at all, so it does not produce as thickly padded a canvas as cross stitch. However, it can be especially useful where bulk is required to be kept to a minimum, as in picture frames, napkin rings, brooches, etc., and in fact for any decorative item where strength and durability are not important. Its other main attributes are that it does not distort the canvas and uses the minimum amount of yarn.

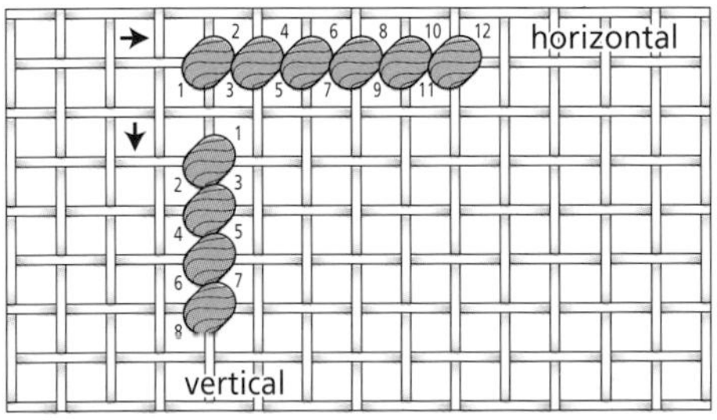

Working half-cross stitch

This stitch resembles tent stitch on the front, but is quite different on the reverse. It is normally stitched in horizontal rows, but can be stitched vertically if the design requires it (Fig 1.12).

Fig 1.12 Half-cross stitch.

4
William Morris-Style Pincushion

This traditional design has been inspired by William Morris's 'Lodden', first seen in 1884 as a printed cotton fabric. The soft pastel colours of stranded cotton selected for the intertwining flowers and leaves create an overall pretty effect with a slight sheen. Cross stitch is an ideal choice for this project, as there is a large number of single stitches and lines. If tent or basketweave had been used, because of their one-directional nature, there would have been the usual problems of non-continuous lines (see page 12 and Fig 1.5 on page 11).

Finished diameter

11cm (4¼in)

You will need

- 18 hpi interlock or mono canvas, white, 21cm (8½in) square
- DMC stranded cotton:
  - 1 skein each of 564, 745, 760, 761, 3713, 3722, 3816, 3817
  - 2 skeins 746
- tapestry needle, size 22
- 2oz (70g) polyester wadding, 10.5cm (4⅛in) square
- one double pincushion with 11cm (4¼in) diameter cushion pad

How to stitch the Pincushion

1 All stitching is carried out in two strands of cotton

2 Fold the canvas in half in both directions, and mark the centre point with a thread or permanent pen.

3 Bind the edges with masking tape or bias binding and attach to a 15cm (6in) embroidery hoop.

Key

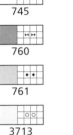

745	746
760	3816
761	3817
3713	564
3722	

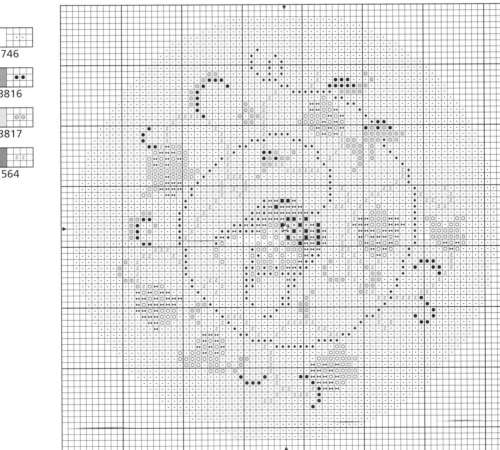

4 Use the centre mark to locate and start stitching the middle flower.

5 Stitch the pink circular stalk, which will then make it easier to position the remaining flowers, leaves, and stems.

6 Finally, fill in the background, starting at the top and working in horizontal rows downwards.

7 Remove from the hoop, and refer to page 125 for attaching to the pincushion.

For best results

- Draw a circle of 11cm (4¼in) diameter on the canvas before attaching to the hoop. This will quickly show where the background stitching stops, rather than counting every row.
- Do not jump from one area to another with the same thread, as this may leave a shadow through the background stitching.

Adapting the design

This design would make a very attractive full-size decorative cushion. The circular pattern could be stitched in the centre, edged with a pink or yellow border. Behind this, the area could be divided into four equal quarters, in which the design would again be stitched (Fig 1.13). To achieve this, use a 10 hpi canvas, and stitch with one strand of tapestry wool.

Fig 1.13 The William Morris design adapted to a square cushion.

5 Rainbow Elephants Pencil Box Lid

This is a fun project depicting the much-loved elephant, highly patterned and in every colour of the rainbow. DMC Broder Medicis wool, which has been used for this project, is a soft, fine crewel wool (that is, a fine 2-ply worsted yarn) and lovely to stitch with. Half-cross stitch is used throughout, making the project quick and easy to stitch. The elephant shape would be ideal for stitching with waste canvas on to backing material (see the chapter on Waste Canvas in Part Two) to be used for furnishings in a child's bedroom or playroom.

Finished size

24 x 8cm (9½ x 3in)

You will need

- 15 hpi interlock canvas, white, 33.5 x 16.5cm (13 x 6½in)
- DMC Broder Medicis:
  - 1 skein each of 8103, 8128, 8817, 8895, 8955, navy
- 2 skeins each of 8026, 8899
- tapestry needle, size 22
- wooden pencil-box with 24 x 8cm (9½ x 3in) cushion pad
- stencil card, brush, and crayons

How to stitch

1 Using three strands of wool in the needle throughout, start by stitching the navy elephant outlines.

2 Stitch the patterns on the elephants next: the red checks, yellow spots, and blue zigzags. Fill in around these.

3 The stars on the elephants' rugs and the background around these should be worked next.

4 Position the navy stars and stitch the green stripes around these.

5 Finally, fill in the three main background colours: blue, pink, and yellow.

6 For attaching to the box lid, refer to page 126.

For best results

If a frame has not been used, lightly press the wrong side of the stitching with a damp cloth to achieve a flatter, smoother appearance.

Stencilling

The elephant theme has been continued with two more stencilled on the inside of the lid (Fig 1.14). Cut the stencil using a craft knife in stencil card and choose favourite colours to paint them in. Attach the stencil to the box with masking tape and colour as preferred, using a small stencil brush and crayons. Refer to the stencilling instructions for the Tropical Leaf Cushion Panel (Project 7).

Fig 1.14 Stencil pattern for inside of lid.

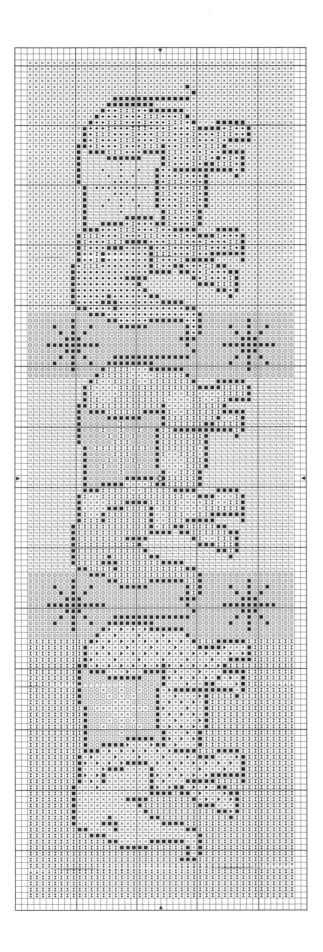

Key

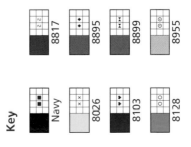

8817
8895
8899
8955
Navy
8026
8103
8128

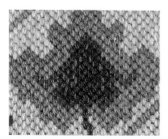

Straight Stitch

Straight stitch is the basic component for a whole group of stitch patterns and variations, each with their own names, but all with a common definition: the stitches lying parallel to the vertical canvas. Throughout the history of needlepoint, upright stitches repeated and arranged to form zigzag patterns have dominated in popularity. The late 16th century, the whole of the 17th, and the early 18th century saw these zigzag patterns, then known as Irish stitch, used for cushions, wall hangings, bed valances, curtains, furniture coverings, as well as smaller items such as purses, knife sheaths, and pincushions. The widespread popularity of this technique was no doubt due both to its ease of working for even the least accomplished needlewoman, and its speed in covering the canvas. It is thought that these zigzag patterns originated in medieval Florence; several examples of Florentine work can be seen in the Victoria and Albert Museum; all worked in silk on fine linen canvas.

Several names are used more or less synonymously to describe these zigzag patterns – Florentine, bargello, Hungarian point, point d'Hongrie, flame stitch – however, there are some accepted differences (see Fig 1.15):

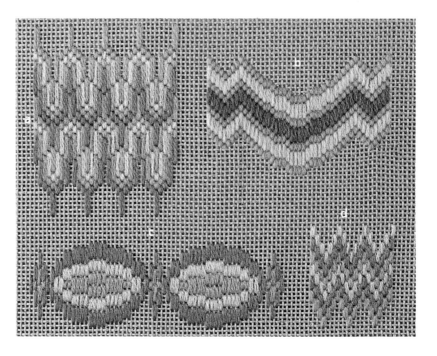

Fig 1.15 Examples of straight stitches.

a   **Hungarian point**
b   **Florentine**
c   **Bargello**
d   **Upright Gobelin**

Upright Gobelin is made up of even-sized stitches in horizontal rows.
Bargello is like upright Gobelin, but worked in steps to move up and down the canvas in rows, creating the traditional flame pattern.
Florentine differs from bargello in that the stitches are a combination of long and short lengths.
Hungarian point or **point d'Hongrie** is worked in rows of single stitches with the characteristic 'point'.

All these repeat patterns rely heavily on the colours used for their effectiveness, as the right colour combinations can add depth and movement to the design. Other straight-stitch patterns are brick stitch, which has been used for the Maple-Leaf project in this chapter, Hungarian stitch, old Florentine stitch, Hungarian diamond, and Parisian stitch (Fig 1.16). Random straight stitch is made up of random-sized stitches not forming any recognizable pattern. This has been adopted in recent years by Kaffe Fassett as one of his favourite stitches, mainly because of its speed in covering the canvas. It has the added advantage of being much more flexible than the other straight stitches as it is not restricted to a regular pattern formation. This, of course, makes it suitable for pictorial designs.

Fig 1.16 Further examples of straight stitches.

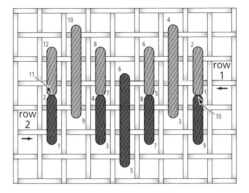

b Hungarian stitch

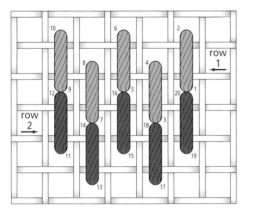

a Brick stitch

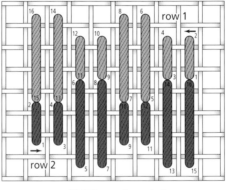

c Old Florentine stitch

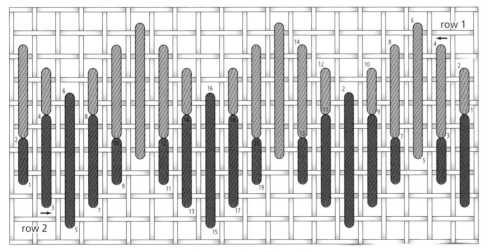

d Hungarian diamond

Fig 1.16 Further examples of straight stitches.

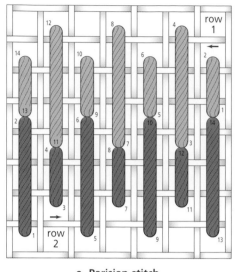

e Parisian stitch

Working straight stitch

It is usually worked over two to six threads in horizontal rows. Each stitch pattern has its own order of work, and it is important to try to adhere to this throughout a project, so that the yarn lying at the back of the work is of a consistent thickness. Interlock canvas is the most suitable for these stitches, as mono canvas threads can sometimes move apart if several stitches start and finish on the same horizontal line. The pairs of threads on double canvas tend to hold the stitches apart, leaving gaps of canvas showing through.

Advantages

- The many possible variations in size and pattern provide opportu nities for innovative work.
- They are quick and easy to stitch, therefore very suitable for large projects and background areas.
- These stitches do not cause distortion of the canvas, so blocking and stretching are unnecessary.
- The canvas back is well covered, making them suitable for items needing to be hard-wearing and durable.
- They can be used in conjunction with other needlepoint stitches, such as tent and basketweave stitch, which adds to their versatility.
- Upright Gobelin is ideal for borders, and especially attractive when trammed to produce a raised effect (see pages 68–9).

Disadvantages

- It is not always easy to select the right thickness of yarn to cover the canvas completely. Too thin a yarn will leave canvas threads showing, while too thick will cause distortion and make even stitching difficult.
- The zigzag-patterned stitches are not suitable for pictorial designs.
- If stitches become very long, this not only affects the durability and hard-wearing qualities of the stitching, but may also cause snagging.

6 Maple Leaf Cushion Panel
in Brick Stitch

This design has been based on the attractive shape and autumn colours of maple leaves. Stitching throughout is over two canvas threads, making it a fairly straightforward project. The thread used is crewel wool, which has been mixed to provide subtle colours and shading. A border of tiny leaves has been provided as an additional feature. Two plain linen fabrics in autumn shades have been selected to complete this project.

Finished size:

A diamond measuring 40cm (16in) across the diagonals.

Finished size of cushion:

41cm (16½in) square.

Stitching the Cushion Panel

1 Fold the canvas in half in both directions and mark the centre. Use this with the centre cross on the chart to position and stitch the central diamond outline. All stitching throughout this project is in brick stitch and uses three strands of crewel wool.

2 Then count the canvas threads to the outer diamond and border edge positions; complete stitching these outlines.

3 Stitch the red leaves, then the green leaves, making sure that the centres of each line up where appropriate.

4 Next, stitch the small leaves in the border, again checking that the centres of alternate leaves line up with the larger ones.

5 Finally, stitch the background.

6 Refer to pages 126–8 for instructions on how to complete this cushion.

For best results

- A frame is not strictly necessary, as distortion of the canvas will not occur; however, it is advisable for an even tension.
- Try not to pull the yarn too tightly, or the canvas threads in between will show through. A slightly looser tension than normal will allow the wool to 'fluff out', helping the canvas coverage.
- Your yarn can be cut in slightly longer lengths than usual, as the larger stitches use it up relatively quickly.

You will need

- 12 hpi interlock canvas, white, 51cm (20in) square
- Appletons' crewel wool:
  - 1 skein each of 254, 475, 476, 722, 864, 865, 866
  - 2 skeins each of 253, 472, 474, 997

- 1 hank 872
- tapestry needle, size 18
- matching fabric to make up the cushion, 50cm (19½in) square
- co-ordinating fabric for the piping and lipping, 50cm (19½in) square
- matching sewing thread

- 2oz (70g) polyester wadding, 41cm (16in) square
- lining fabric, 44cm (16½in) square
- zip, 36cm (14in) long
- feather cushion pad, 41cm (16in) square
- 1.8m (5ft) medium piping cord

Adapting the design

This pattern could very easily be extended to cover the complete cushion front, because it is a regular repeat pattern. Alternatively, the border with the small leaves, could be repeated several times to fill up the triangular area. These leaves could be stitched in different colours to match the larger central leaves (Fig 1.17).

Fig 1.17 The Maple Leaf design adapted to a square panel.

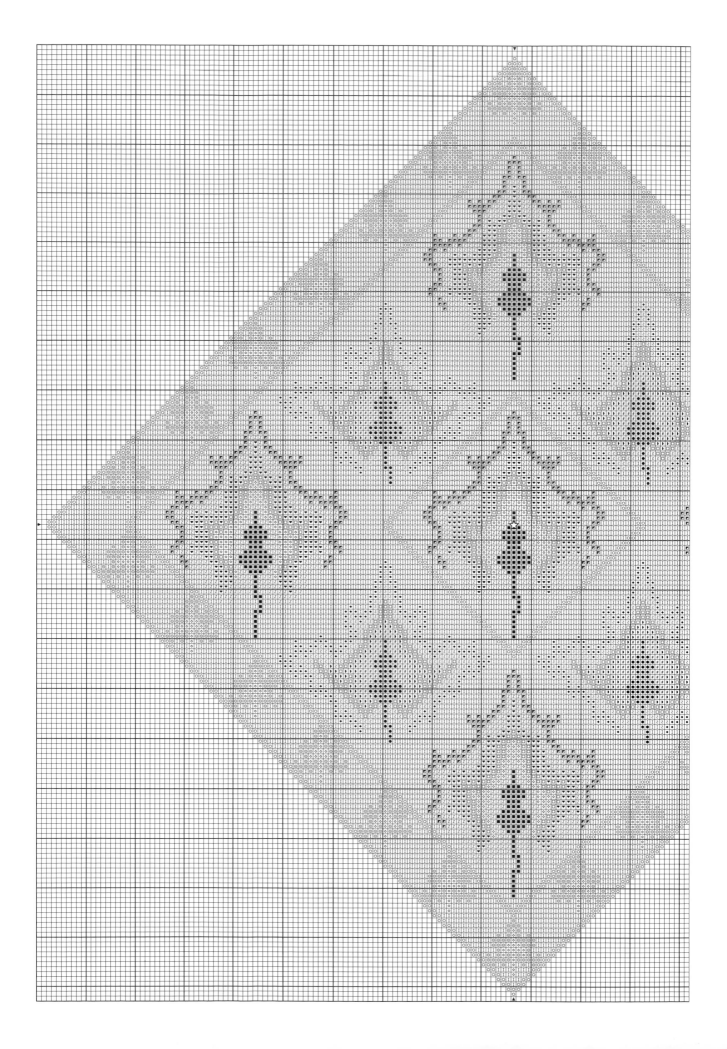

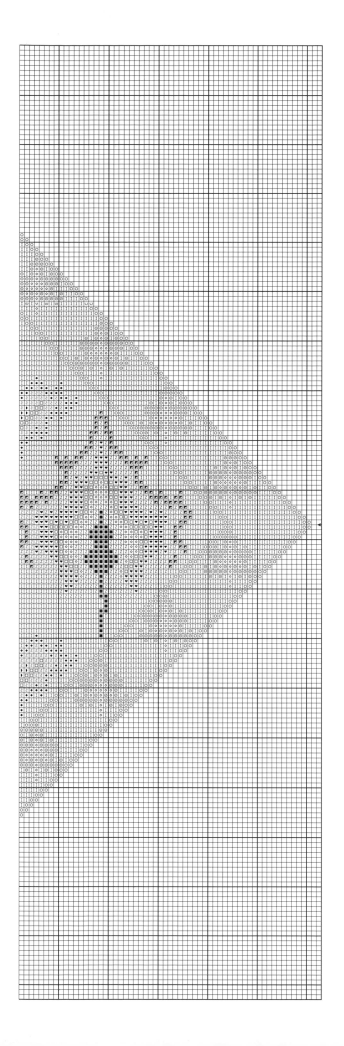

Key

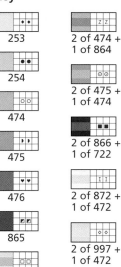

253

254

474

475

476

865

2 of 472 +
1 of 474

2 of 474 +
1 of 864

2 of 475 +
1 of 474

2 of 866 +
1 of 722

2 of 872 +
1 of 472

2 of 997 +
1 of 472

1 of 253 +
1 of 472 +
1 of 997

NB: Since brick stitch over
two threads is used
throughout, each stitch is
represented by *two* symbols.

Part Two Advanced
Stitching Techniques

Crewel Wool Shading

Crewel wool is a fine 2-ply twisted worsted yarn, used for needlepoint since the 17th century. The technique of using more than one colour of wool in the needle at the same time opens up a whole new area for needlepoint enthusiasts. Subtle shadings from one colour to another, or one shade to another, can be achieved. It is a method particularly suitable for the stitching of natural objects such as flowers, leaves, sea, sky, shells, animals, birds, etc., where a three-dimensional effect is required. Light and dark areas on any object can be effectively interpreted, as can readily be seen in the Tropical Leaf project in this chapter.

Crewel wool mixing can also provide added interest to an area that otherwise would have been a solid colour. Backgrounds are ideal for this technique, as can be seen in the Repeat-Patterned Glasses Case, Maple Leaf Cushion, and Georgian Seat Cover (Projects 3, 6, and 11). The Flower Needlecase and the Flower and Fish Chair Seat (Projects 1 and 2) have highlights of blue and apricot within the creamy background. Taking this mixture one step further, intensively mottled effects can be achieved by mixing sharply contrasting colours.

From the 17th century onwards, crewel wool was an ideal yarn for needlepoint because of the finer canvases used, the vast range of decorative stitches worked, and the practice of combining silk with wool in a piece of work. It is very difficult to ascertain whether different shades of colours were mixed together in the needle, because of the general wear and faded nature of much antique needlepoint. However, when the level of skill and patience of the earlier needlewomen is considered, it would seem quite likely. In Victorian times the importation of the new soft, thicker yarn for Berlin wool work, and the subsequent popularity of this style, brought about a decline in the use of crewel wool for needlepoint for many years. The Paterna yarn was developed early this century, and Appletons first produced crewel wool in 1946; only 100 colours were then available, whereas now the range of 420 is exported world-wide.

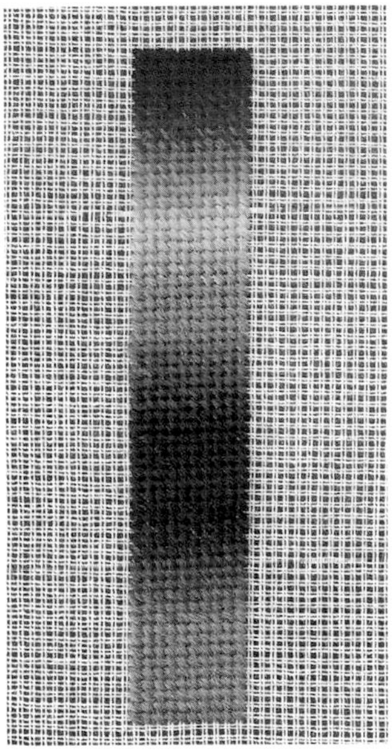

Stitching crewel wool shading

It is a good idea to try out the crewel wool shading technique by stitching a small sample. Select a light, medium, and dark shade of one colour, and stitch a block using each of the following combinations for two rows.

Start with
- three strands of light
- two strands light, one medium
- one strand light, two medium
- three medium
- two medium, one dark
- one medium, two dark;

finish with
- three dark.

The stitched rainbow smoothly progressing through the entire spectrum of colour illustrates this technique effectively (see Fig 2.1).

Canvas

The number of strands of crewel wool to be used must be determined according to the gauge size of the canvas and the stitches selected; see the table below.

Fig 2.1 A rainbow of shaded colours.

Threads

The three brands most readily available are Appletons' crewel, the finer DMC Broder Medicis, and the loosely twisted Paterna yarn, which is a 3-ply thickness that can be divided into single strands. A comparison of these is included in the table on page 2.

Needles

Use the appropriate size for the canvas gauge selected, as usual.

Stitches

Crewel work is suitable for all the basic stitches, and is especially ideal for the decorative ones, as anything from 1 to 6 strands can be used in the needle, depending on the thickness of thread required.

Method

The required numbers of strands in the selected colours are threaded through the needle together. Try to keep the strands untwisted, so that the stitches will lie completely flat on the canvas. If they become twisted it will be particularly noticeable if strands of contrasting colour are included. Care must also be taken to ensure that one strand does not slip through the needle, as this will create loose loops on the stitches.

Stitching with Crewel Wool

Canvas hpi   Recommended number of strands

Canvas hpi	Appletons' Crewel			DMC Broder Medicis			Paterna Persian (1 strand)		
	Tent/ Basket	Cross stitch	Straight stitch	Tent/ Basket	Cross stitch	Straight stitch	Tent/ Basket	Cross stitch	Straight stitch
10	4	3	4	5	3	5	3	1	2
12	3	2	3–4	4	2	4	2	1	2
14	3	1	3	3	2	3	1	1	2
16	2	1	2	2	1	2	1	–	1

45

7 Tropical Leaf Cushion Panel

To make up into a flanged-edge cushion, overall size 51cm (20in) square, a 41cm (16in) cushion pad will be required.

A visit to a local rainforest garden supplied the ideal source material for this project. *Anthurium magnificum columbia* is the name of this spectacular foliage, with leaves up to about 30cm (12in) in size. Although the leaves are basically green in colour with their characteristic creamy veins, closer inspection reveals subtle integrated yellow and blue-grey areas. Crewel wool is perfect for capturing these colour variations. The position of the light source is an important element in this project. Not only is there more light on the leaves at the front of the group, but also on the right-hand side; this additional light is also reflected in the stitching shades. The panel has been made up into an attractive conservatory cushion, using lightly sponged calico which has also been stencilled with *Anthurium magnificum columbia* leaf shapes in subtle shades of yellow, green, and blue.

Finished size

20 x 18cm (8 x 7in).

How to stitch the Leaf Panel

1 Draw a 15cm (6in) square on the canvas with a permanent marker pen, and mark the centre position.

2 Attach to a small frame and use three strands of crewel wool throughout, and half-cross stitch.

3 Start stitching in all the veins on the leaves, using the centre mark to help to position them correctly.

4 Complete the front leaf first, then the others in the order shown in Fig 2.2.

5 After all the leaves have been stitched, the colour patches in the background should be put in, using either two strands of 351 with one of 992, or two of 872 with one of 992. These have been placed in a totally random pattern, and can be increased or altered depending on personal preference.

6 Finally stitch in the background, working from the top of the canvas down to the bottom.

7 Remove from the frame, and make up into a cushion using the instructions on pages 128–30.

For best results

• As many of the colours used are only very slightly different, they can

Fig 2.2 Order of stitching.

You will need

• 14 hpi mono or interlock canvas, white, 26cm (10in) square
• Appletons' crewel wool:
  • 1 skein each of 151,157, 251A, 252, 351, 543, 551, 552, 641, 872, 873, 876, 987
  • 2 skeins each of 155, 293, 403
  • 1 hank 992
• tapestry needle, size 20

• matching cream calico fabric, 70cm (28in) square
• matching sewing thread
• stencil card
• stencil crayons: yellow, blue, white
• stencil brush, small or medium size
• yellow-green fabric paint
• small natural sponge

• Madeira rayon machine embroidery thread (Art. no. 9840, no. 40–200m), nos. 1067, 1100
• 2 oz (70g) polyester wadding, 41cm (16in) square
• cream zip, 35cm (14in)
• feather cushion pad, 41cm (16in) square

Fig 2.3 Stencil pattern for cushion border.

easily become mixed up, especially when making up the colour combinations required. Try to find a means of keeping them all separate, such as a tray with separate compartments, a large number of small paper or polythene bags or a palette with large holes. This will save a great deal of time throughout the entire project.

• As there are a large number of colour changes within one leaf, it will be quite easy to lose your place when working from the chart. Use one of the methods suggested in the Introduction to reduce the risk of this.

• Use several needles, each with a different combination of colours, to cut down threading time.

Sponging and stencilling

1 Cut the calico to 65cm (26in) square, pre-wash, dry, and iron before starting to sponge and stencil; this will remove dressing in the fabric which can make it non-receptive to certain paints. Measure a 12cm (4¾in) border all round, which will not be stencilled on.

2 Pour a little of the fabric paint onto a saucer and add some water to make a pale mixture. Try this out on a sample of fabric first; it should be pale enough not to interfere with the stencilling, but not so light that it cannot be seen. When satisfied with the colour, cover the fabric with it, using a natural sponge. Try to turn the sponge in different directions, so that the same pattern does not keep repeating itself.

3 When this is dry, heat-set with a warm to hot iron.

4 Using the stencil outlines (Fig 2.3), trace onto a stencil card and cut out the appropriate sections with a craft knife. If a cut is accidentally made in the wrong position, place masking tape over both sides of the card and recut.

5 Fig 2.4 shows the layout used here for the leaves; this, of course, could be altered if preferred.

Fig 2.4 Layout of stencilled border.

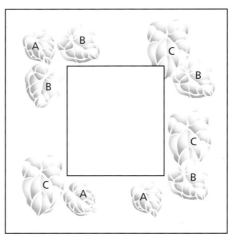

6 Taking the three stencil crayons, rub a small amount of each onto a palette. Mix a green colour with the blue and yellow, and test all the colours on a sample of calico.

7 Before starting to stencil, mark the position of the central needlepoint square with pins. Select the leaves which are lying underneath others and stencil these first, using masking tape to secure to the calico. Use the tape also for protecting the calico where two leaves are close together.

8 The leaves in the photographed version have been shaded, so that they are bluer in the bottom left-hand corner, and particularly light and yellow in the middle and bottom right-hand side.

9 Several of the leaves have been reversed to give greater variation; remember to clean the stencil with white spirit before turning it over.

10 Leave the stencilled fabric to dry for a day or two before further handling.

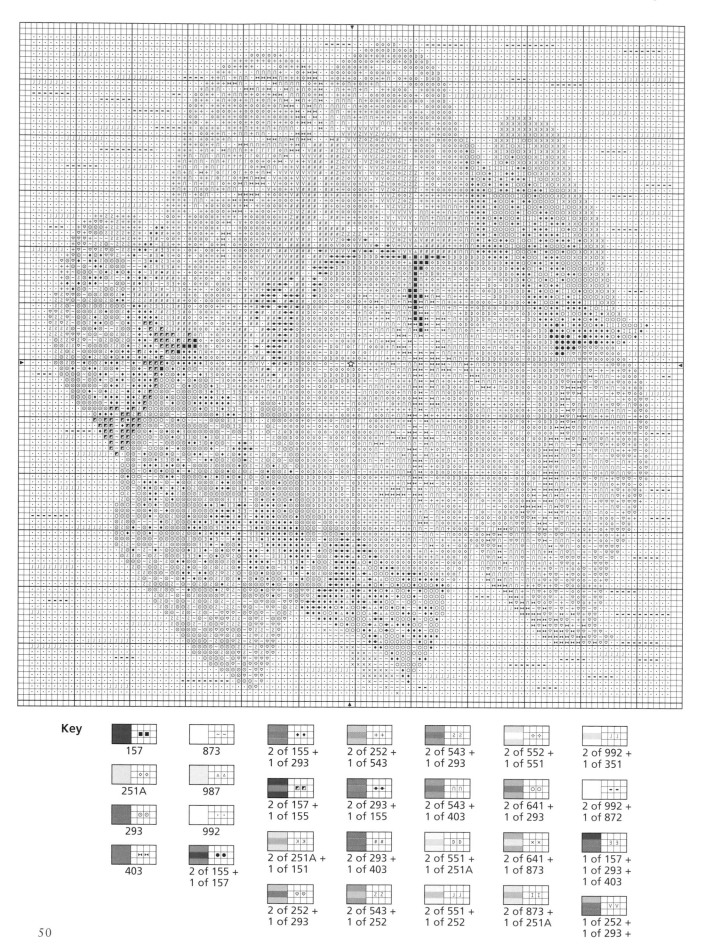

Key

157	873	2 of 155 + 1 of 293	2 of 252 + 1 of 543	2 of 543 + 1 of 293	2 of 552 + 1 of 551	2 of 992 + 1 of 351
251A	987	2 of 157 + 1 of 155	2 of 293 + 1 of 155	2 of 543 + 1 of 403	2 of 641 + 1 of 293	2 of 992 + 1 of 872
293	992	2 of 251A + 1 of 151	2 of 293 + 1 of 403	2 of 551 + 1 of 251A	2 of 641 + 1 of 873	1 of 157 + 1 of 293 + 1 of 403
403	2 of 155 + 1 of 157	2 of 252 + 1 of 293	2 of 543 + 1 of 252	2 of 551 + 1 of 252	2 of 873 + 1 of 251A	1 of 252 + 1 of 293 + 1 of 403

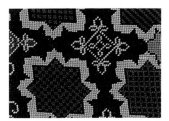

Decorative Stitches

There are a vast number of stitches that can be used in needlepoint, varying not only in their size and shape, but also in the texture and pattern created. Many have been used for centuries and are beautifully illustrated in early samplers, whilst others are the innovative results of today's designers.

favourite, both for small items such as purses and for large-scale pieces such as the Hatton Garden Panels. Florentine work then took over, especially for large furnishing items, whilst the Victorian era used very few decorative stitches, except for plush stitch, often seen in conjunction with Berlin wool work (Fig 2.5b). Throughout this century the

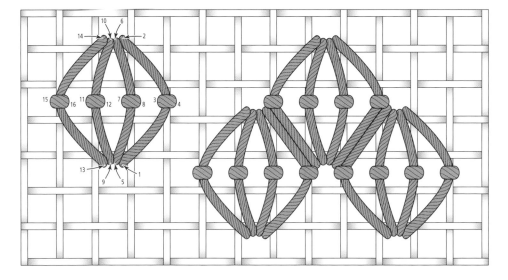

Fig 2.5 Examples of decorative stitches.

a Rococo stitch. The stitches can be of considerable length, but will remain stable because of the small horizontal securing stitches. It is usually best to complete each group before proceeding to the next.

All the stitches are variations and adaptations of four basic types: vertical, diagonal, cross, and composite. Over the centuries, stitches, just like needlepoint techniques, have enjoyed periods of popularity and decline. In the 17th century Gobelin stitches were used extensively, primarily to imitate woven tapestry (the stitch takes its name from the Gobelin tapestry factory in Paris); whilst at the turn of the century rococo stitch (see Fig 2.5a) became a great

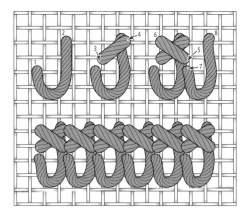

b Plush stitch. Loops of thread approximately 2cm (¾in) long are held in place by cross stitches. When the whole area has been stitched, the loops are cut and may then be clipped to the required length.

emphasis on good design has encouraged the use of many decorative stitches, with their scope for experimentation and unusual variations.

The main reason for using these ornamental stitches is to create texture, which in turn creates added tonal interest and excitement in a piece of work. Interesting lines and patterns can be formed by the arrangement of some stitches, whilst others form a raised, padded effect. Designers have also adopted particular stitches in order to help interpret the physical properties of a specific design element – for example, vertical stitches such as Gobelin and Hungarian for brickwork, walls and roofs, or composite stitches such as Leviathan and Rhodes for flowers and foliage (Fig 2.5c and d). Needlepoint

which uses very many decorative stitches usually has a less detailed pictorial design than that which consists wholly of tent stitch. This is because decorative stitches are not generally suitable for minute details and complex shading, and also because a highly complex pictorial design with numerous different colours, as well as decorative stitches, can be confusing.

An appropriate use for them today is in the stitching of background areas. Instead of an area of solid colour in tent stitch, a more interesting texture can be achieved by using a decorative stitch, as can be seen in the Ship design (Project 17).

Another reason for using these stitches is the speed with which the canvas can be covered. This certainly has been a major factor in the use of Florentine work in the 18th century, both for large sets of chairs and for extensive wall hangings.

Working decorative stitches

Canvas

Mono or interlock canvas is normally the most suitable for these stitches, as double canvas can be confusing where there is a great deal of thread-counting. As the threads on mono canvas are less secure than on interlock, this too can occasionally cause problems with threads moving, especially if the yarn is pulled tightly over several of them.

The mesh size of the canvas must be selected carefully to suit both the stitches and thickness of yarn being used. Too fine a canvas will result in the stitches being tiny and tight, with the component parts being just a blur; while too coarse a canvas will result in bare

Fig 2.5 Examples of decorative stitches.

c Leviathan stitch can be worked over any even number of threads, and each unit should be completed before proceeding to the next one.

d Rhodes stitch can be worked over any even number of threads, and can be either square or oblong.

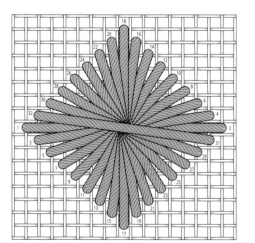

canvas threads showing through the yarn strands. Many of these composite stitches do not cover the canvas completely, and in fact this may be used as a design feature. It is a good idea to use a coloured canvas, as for the Picture Frame project in this chapter, or to colour the canvas first with thinned acrylic paints.

Threads

These stitches provide an excellent opportunity to experiment with some of the exciting new threads available; silks, rayons, linens, cottons, synthetics, and metallic, as well as the more traditional wools. Many have a glossy sheen, which can be utilized effectively, creating both shadow patterns and colour variations. However, it is important to remember the function of the piece of needlepoint, and how much strength and durability will be required of it. If it is expected to stand up to constant use and wear for the next 100 years, then a reputable woollen yarn is almost certainly the best choice.

Needles

Use the appropriate size for the canvas selected (see the table on page 3).

Stitches

These vary enormously in their coverage of both the right and wrong sides of the canvas, which in turn will affect the strength and longevity of a piece of work. Generally, the more 'open' the stitch, the less hard-wearing it will be, and the smaller the stitch, the stronger it will be. Coverage of the wrong side of the canvas is an additional factor to consider; for example, a trammed stitch (see pages 68–9) will create more padding and ultimately adds to a canvas's wearing qualities.

Method

Each stitch will have its own method of working. These have been devised for a variety of reasons: evenness of tension, ease of remembering, coverage of the wrong side of the canvas, economical use of yarn, or speed. As we saw in the case of cross stitch (page 26), Method 1 created an even appearance, Method 2 left more yarn on the wrong side for padding, and Method 3 was the quickest. For many of the stitches used in the Rug project in this chapter, the chosen method is the one which uses the most vertical and horizontal stitches on the wrong side, rather than diagonal stitches, in order to minimize the amount of distortion that may occur. This is always an important consideration for rugs, as they are difficult to block back to shape because of their weight and size.

To try out some of the stitches included in this chapter, make your own arrangement on a small square of canvas. Different threads, such as cotton, wool, or metallic, could be used, and the size of the stitches varied. When completed, this could be made up into a pincushion or the front of a needlecase.

Projects

Two very different projects have been included in this section to illustrate a wide range of decorative stitches. For the Picture Frame, the stitches were chosen purely for their visual effect, whereas for the Rug this aspect had to go hand in hand with the requirement for durability. The large-mesh canvas, together with the wool thickness, also imposed limitations on the final stitch choice.

8 Picture Frame

A selection of traditional needle-point stitches has been given a modern interpretation by the use of rayon machine embroidery threads. The variation in texture created by the stitches effectively utilizes the lovely sheen of the threads, producing an overall shimmering effect. An added advantage of such threads is that a varying number of strands can be used, as required by the different stitches.

Finished size

18 x 22.2cm external (7 x 8¾in),
9 x 12.5cm internal (3½ x 5in),
4.5cm frame width (1¾in)

How to stitch

1 Fold the canvas into four and mark the centre thread, then attach to a frame in the usual way. Note that the chart shows only a quarter of the total design, so to make the whole frame you will need to repeat the pattern in each of the four quarters of the canvas; remember that two quarters will need to be a mirror image of the other two.

2 Use the chart to determine which stitch to use, and refer to the key for the number of strands of thread needed.

3 Measure 4.5cm (1¾in) from the centre mark upwards, and 6.25cm (2½in) outwards, to give the upper left-hand corner of the inner opening of the frame.

4 Stitch the line of triangles in satin stitch, and then the line of Florentine zigzags above them (see Fig 2.6a–b). Once those two are complete, the positioning of the other three sides will be easy.

You will need

- 22 hpi mono canvas, yellow, 28 x 32cm (11 x 12½in)
- Madeira rayon machine embroidery thread (Art no. 9840, no. 40, 200m): 1 reel each of 1045, 1279, 2101, 2103
- 2oz (70g) polyester wadding, 18 x 22cm (7 x 8¾in)
- 1 piece of strong cardboard, 18 x 22cm (7 x 8¾in)
- 1 piece of thin card, 18 x 22cm (7 x 8¾in)
- strong crochet cotton for lacing
- matching backing fabric, 21 x 25cm (8¼ x 9¾in)

Fig 2.6 Decorative stitches for the Picture Frame.

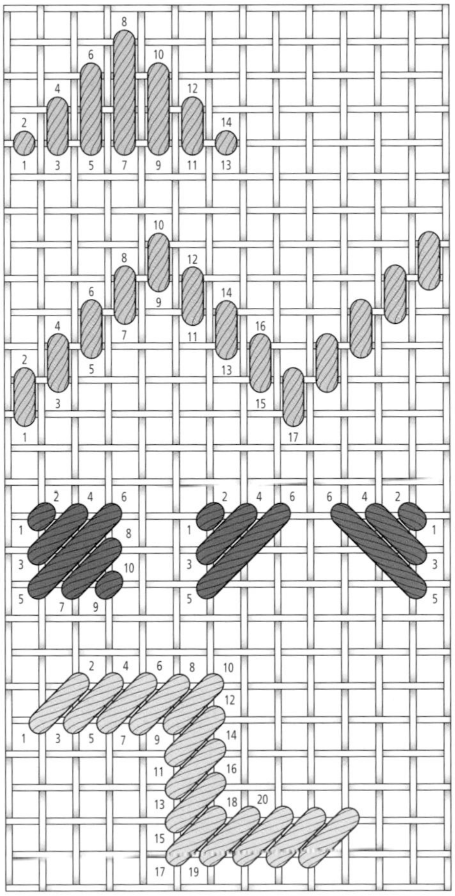

a Satin stitch triangles

b Florentine zigzags

c Cushion and half-cushion

d Byzantine stitch

Chart 8 key

Stitch	Number of strands used	Number of canvas threads stitched over	Colour
1 Satin	8	2–4	1045
2 Florentine	8	4	1045
3 Small half-cushion	6	1–4	1270
4 Large half-cushion	6	1–7	1270
5 Rhodes	4	16	2103
6 Byzantine	6	3	2101
7 Florentine	8	3	1045
8 Satin	8	2–6	1270

5 Move gradually outwards, finishing the complete oblong of one stitch before moving on to the next type of stitch. This will act as a check that mistakes have not been made.

6 In turn, complete the two half-cushion stitches (Fig 2.6c), Rhodes stitch (see Fig 2.5d on page 52), and then the outer row of zigzags and triangles, leaving the Byzantine until last (Fig 2.6d). This is because the filling-in of incomplete stitches, in areas where there is not room for the decorative stitch to be worked in full, is made much easier if outlines are in position first. (Any empty spaces in the area of Byzantine stitch should be filled in with tent stitch.)

7 Remember when stitching the diamonds of Rhodes stitch that the starting position must be exactly the same each time, so that the final threads will all lie in the same direction.

8 Remove from the frame and refer to pages 130–1.

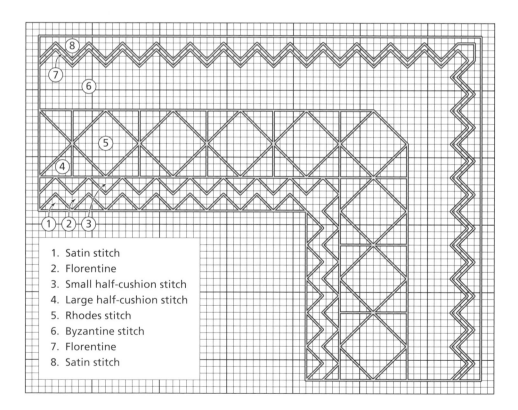

1. Satin stitch
2. Florentine
3. Small half-cushion stitch
4. Large half-cushion stitch
5. Rhodes stitch
6. Byzantine stitch
7. Florentine
8. Satin stitch

9 Rug with Decorative Panels

This rug has been based on ancient Islamic geometric patterns, which are to be found throughout the Islamic world, in architecture, textiles, calligraphy, metalwork, etc. The ban by Muslim law on the representation of living creatures meant that geometry was always highly important in the area of design.

The 14 star shapes in the rug have provided an ideal opportunity to display several decorative stitches. However, these have been limited to the relatively small ones for practical purposes. Oblong cross stitch has been selected for the border edge, as it provides a tough, hardwearing surface. Basketweave stitch has been used throughout except for the decorative stitch areas, in order to minimize any distortion of the canvas.

Finished size
109 x 72cm (43 x 28½in)

You will need

- 7 hpi sudan canvas (a sized canvas from DMC), ecru, 125 x 87cm (49 x 34in)
- DMC tapestry wool:
  - 37 skeins 7370
  - 59 skeins 7453
  - 42 skeins 7590
  - 46 skeins 7591
- 41 skeins 7356
- 46 skeins 7127
- tapestry needle, size 16
- close weave hessian for backing, 117 x 80cm (46 x 31in)
- strong beige linen thread
- small curved needle

How to stitch
1 Mark the centre thread of the canvas and extend lines out so as the centre of each side is also marked. These will act as a useful checking mechanism when the design is being stitched. Note that the chart shows only a quarter of the total design, so to make the whole rug you will need to repeat the pattern in each of the four quarters of the canvas; remember that two quarters will need to be a mirror image of the other two.

2 Attach to a frame.

3 Use double tapestry wool throughout.

4 The following list is the order of stitching. As it is quite unlikely that your frame will be large enough to stitch the entire rug, it will have to be worked in several sections. Taking each section in turn, complete it entirely using the listed order:
- beige lines in the centre pattern
- navy star outlines
- beige outline borders
- beige patterns in the red crosses.

Contintental tent stitch

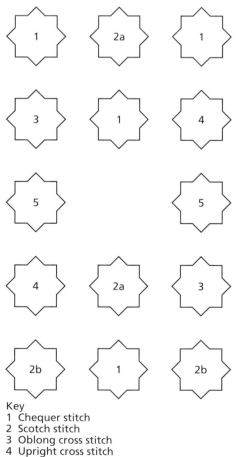

Fig 2.7 Arrangement of the decorative panels.

Key
1 Chequer stitch
2 Scotch stitch
3 Oblong cross stitch
4 Upright cross stitch
5 Chequer stitch variation

Fig 2.8 Decorative stitches for the Rug.

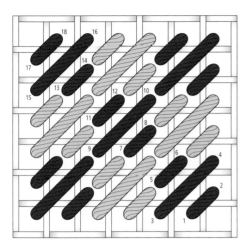

- Fill in the navy, blue, red, and green areas in the centre pattern using basketweave stitch.
- Stitch the stars using the appropriate decorative stitch for each. (Fig 2.7 shows which decorative stitch is used for each star; Fig 2.8 gives instructions for each type of stitch.) These have all been worked in orange and red wools. Then complete:
- red outlines around the stars using continental tent stitch

a. **Chequer stitch.** Work diagonally across the star shape in alternating rows of orange and red.

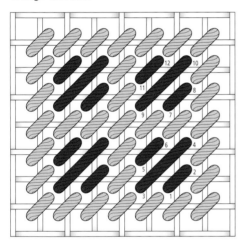

b. **Scotch stitch.** Begin by working chequer stitches in vertical or horizontal rows. Panels 2a have red chequer stitches surrounded by orange tent stitches; panels 2b have the colours reversed.

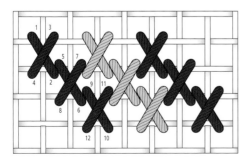

c. **Oblong cross stitch.** Work in diagonal rows of alternating red and orange.

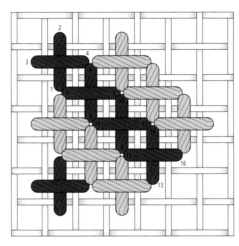

d. **Upright cross stitch.** Work in diagonal rows of alternating red and orange.

e. **Chequer stitch variation.** Work in horizontal rows of alternating orange and red.

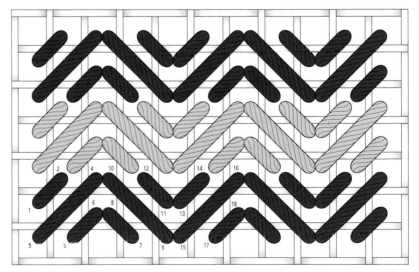

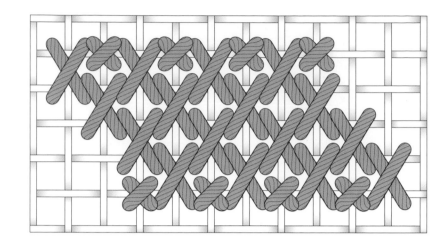

Fig 2.8
f. Green border edging.
After the rows of oblong cross stitch have been completed, fill in the gaps along both edges with a simple cross stitch.

Basketweave stitch
- beige area around the stars
- red star areas
- blue border areas
- orange border areas
- navy border areas
- green border areas
- green border edge using oblong cross stitch (Fig 2.8f).

5 Remove from the frame and refer to page 131 for finishing instructions.

Joining the canvas

If the frame you have available is not large enough to accommodate the size of the canvas required for this project, then it is quite satisfactory to stitch the design in two smaller pieces and join them afterwards. Make this join to the left or right of the centre of the rug, so that the decorative stitches are not included. The overlap of the join will be five stitches.

1 Decide on which five lines are to be overlapped, and leave these unstitched on the left side of one piece, and the right side of the other.

Key

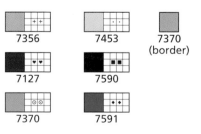

7356	7453	7370 (border)
7127	7590	
7370	7591	

Star shapes: 7146 and 7198, as shown in Fig 2.8

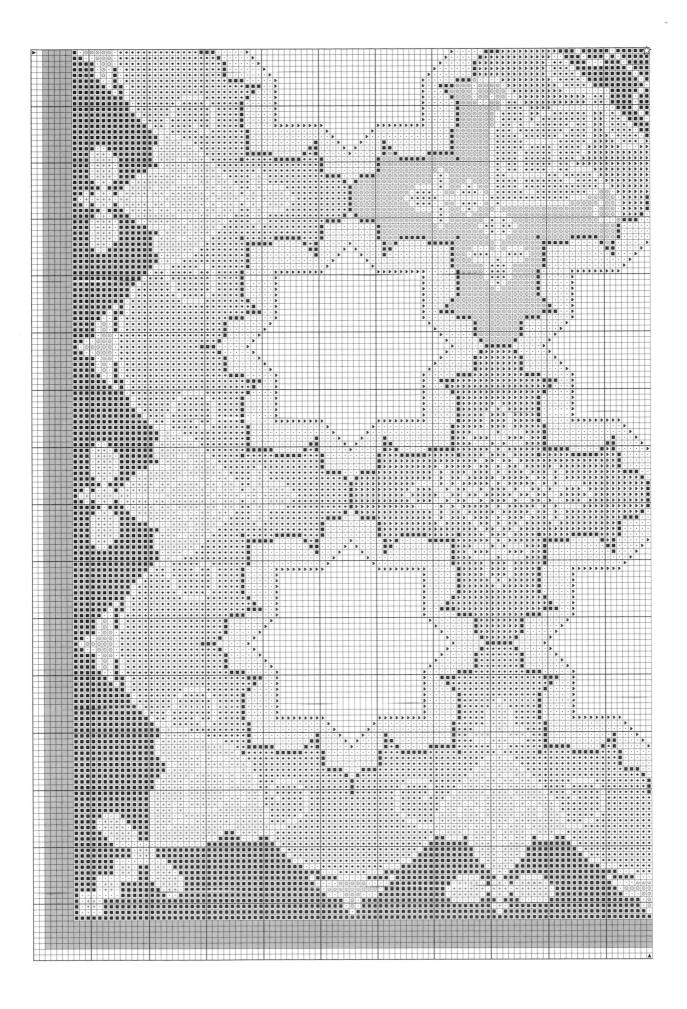

2 Trim the canvas on both pieces after the fifth canvas thread. Make this cut accurately between two threads of canvas and proceed with the join straight away. If the cut edges are left for any length of time, treat them with Fraycheck.

3 Overlap the two sections, matching up the canvas holes and threads carefully. Pin in position, and backstitch two lines using every hole (Fig 2.9). Use a cream sewing thread to match the canvas colour.

4 Stitch the appropriate stitch over this join, matching up the surrounding colour and pattern. When complete, the join will not be visible except for a slightly raised effect.

Fig 2.9 Joining the canvas.

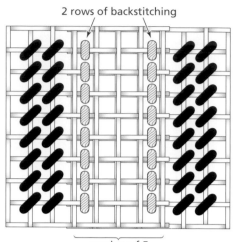

2 rows of backstitching

overlap of 5 canvas threads

Petit Point

Petit point is simply half-cross stitch or continental tent stitch, worked on a fine-gauge canvas, 16 hpi or above. It is used where minute details and intricate shading are required, as in faces, figures, or busy and complicated scenes. **Mille-point** is a very fine petit point usually worked in silk on a silk gauze, which is then applied to a larger-gauge canvas, where petit point and **gros point** (stitches worked over two canvas threads) are worked around it. Mille-point, with its hundred or more stitches to the inch, can give an incredible depth of detail, but tends to be seldom seen because of its obvious disadvantages of being very time-consuming, and very difficult to see to work.

Historically petit point was a pursuit of the leisured class, as only they could afford the time, or money for the silk and wools. An inventory of Mary, Queen of Scots' possessions in 1586 includes an unfinished panel of '124 birds of different kinds in petit point'. The 17th century saw a large number of small pieces worked in petit point, usually 30 or more holes to the inch, such as jewellery boxes, caskets, and mirror surrounds. Small worked pieces of petit point were also used for larger items by appliquéing them onto a fine background fabric; these were called **slips**. Examples can be seen at Glamis Castle, Angus, where linen bed hangings display petit-point birds, animals, and stylized flower motifs, and at Blair Castle, Perthshire, where satin bed hangings display beautifully stitched fish and mythical creatures with floral swags.

Towards the end of the 17th and throughout the 18th century, an increasing use of fully upholstered furniture led to an enormous demand for canvas-work coverings, for chairs, sofas, and settees. Many floral designs in petit point covered entire sets of chairs, but more often panels, as fine as 40 holes per inch or more, depicting mythical or pastoral subjects, were surrounded by gros point. Fine examples can be seen at Montacute, Clandon Park, Canons Ashby House (all National Trust properties), and at the Victoria and Albert Museum, where panels of petit point depict scenes from Gay's Fables.

The 19th century saw the introduction of the very popular, heavier Berlin wools, which were unsuitable for petit point; however, the development of Penelope double canvas, and the introduction of several fine-gauge canvases, ensured its continuation. A 20th-century example of the partnership between petit point and

gros point can be seen at Standon House, West Sussex, which was built by Philip Webb, with furnishings by William Morris. The set of Arts and Crafts-style dining chairs depicts various mythical beasts in petit point, surrounded by stylized leaf borders in gros point.

Working petit point

Canvas

The most readily available mono or interlock canvases for petit point are 18 and 22 hpi, available in white, antique, and a few pastel shades. Penelope double canvas is ideal for working petit point and gros point together, and offers a wide range of sizes to choose from: 7 hpi (14, using all the holes, for petit point) up to 20 hpi (40 for petit point). For even finer work, silk gauze can be used, starting at 24 hpi, and going up to 112 hpi.

Threads

Crewel wool is generally used for petit point. The readily available ones are Appletons', Paterna, Twilley's, and DMC's Broder Medicis. Stranded cottons may also be used: one strand is fine enough to work up to 40 hpi, and above this silk threads are recommended. The table below provides a guide to the number of strands of crewel wool needed for different gauges of canvas.

Needles

Use size 22 for 18 and 20 hpi; size 24 for 20, 22, and 24 hpi; and size 26 for finer gauges.

Method

Work exactly as for continental tent stitch, following all the suggestions given in the Introduction for a professional finish. It is particularly important when stitching petit point that the needle and thread are not too thick for the canvas gauge, as any distortion will lead to uneven and irregular stitches. For the finer petit point, especially when using silk gauze, half-cross is preferable to continental tent, as the bulk and padding created by the latter on the wrong side would be inappropriate. When using double canvas, simply push the pairs of threads apart, so that stitching can be worked over single threads. If a piece of work requires petit point and gros point together, stitch all of the petit-point designs first, then fill in the background with the gros point, working as closely as possible up to the petit point. Finally, fill in any gaps between the two, by using the same thickness of yarn as the petit point, but in the gros-point colours.

Stitching in Petit Point

Canvas hpi	Recommended number of strands			
	Appletons'	Twilley's	Paterna	DMC Broder Medicis
16–18	2	1	1	2
22	1	–	–	1
30	–	–	–	1

10 Victorian Dolls' House Carpet

This carpet is to a scale of 1/12 of full size, making it perfect for dolls' house collectors. As there are now many styles of Victorian houses and every conceivable item of furniture and household article to collect, it seemed appropriate to design such a carpet. It is especially typical of that era, not only because of its cabbage-type roses, but also because of the Victorians' great love of needlepoint.

Finished size

10.5 x 17cm (4¼ x 6¾in)

You will need

- 18 hpi white canvas, 20 x 27cm (8 x 10½in)
- Appletons' crewel wool:
  1 skein each of 151, 225, 227, 252, 353, 403, 604, 754, 877, 941
- tapestry needle, size 24

How to stitch the Carpet

1 Attach to a small frame in the usual way, mark the centre, and use one strand of crewel wool and half-cross stitch throughout. The one strand of wool is too thin by normal standards, but here it will produce a slightly threadbare look. It will also, in conjunction with the half-cross stitch, keep the bulk of wool to a minimum, which is essential for creating an even surface for the furniture to stand on.
2 Start stitching the central spray of roses and then the lilac trellis lines. Once these are in position, the rest of the rose sprays can be completed.
3 Next, stitch the inner and outer green border lines, before filling in with the roses.
4 Remove from the frame and finish according to the instructions on page 131.

For best results

- For all stitching, complete areas of colour rather than full lines.
- Avoid jumping from one area to another with a continuous thread, unless it is only 2 or 3 threads away.
- Take care when finishing threads on the wrong side that long ends are not left, as these might be pulled through to the right side with subsequent stitching.

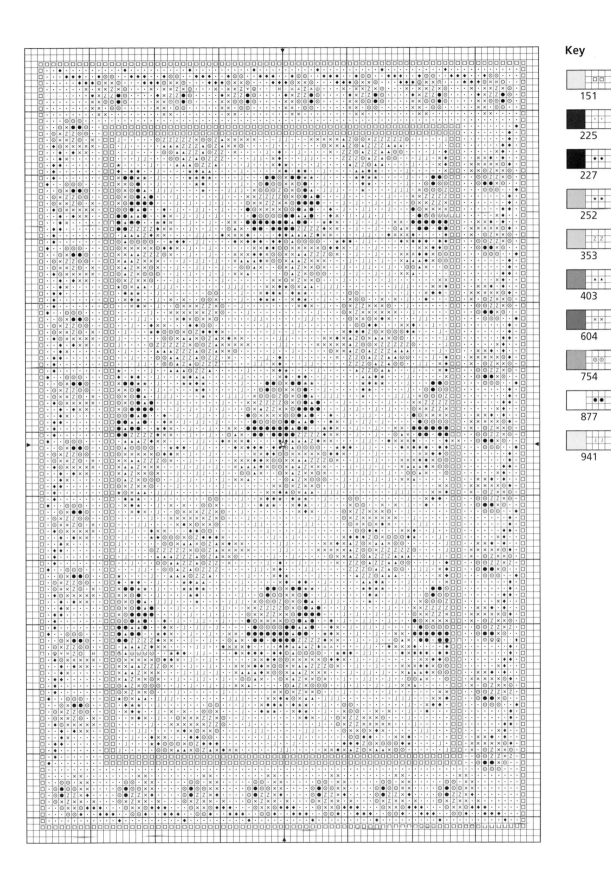

Key

151

225

227

252

353

403

604

754

877

941

Tramming

Tramming is the technique of laying long lengths of yarn across the weft of the canvas, in the correct colour for the design. These threads are normally laid between the narrow pairs of double-canvas threads, before being worked over, usually in half-cross stitch, continental tent, or straight stitch. Tramming, or **trame** in American usage, seems to have originated from *tram*, a word used instead of 'weft' in the weaving of good-quality silk. When tramming was first used in needlepoint, its main function was to create extra padding for warmth and durability. However, by Victorian times, it seems to have been used in conjunction with stitches normally associated with poor canvas coverage. Mrs Beeton's *Book of Needlework*, originally published in 1870, recommends the use of thin cord or thick wool as a tramming thread for upright Gobelin or straight stitch.

Today tramming is used for three main reasons:
- As a means of marking the design on the canvas. In this case, the complete design is trammed using the same colours as for the overstitching. Those commercial kits which use this method are in fact the easiest to stitch, as charts are unnecessary and there are none of the problems normally associated with painted canvases, such as deciding which colour to use for a particular stitch. However, these kits are generally more costly because of the extra preparation involved.
- To create a raised effect in the trammed areas, in comparison to the flatter, non-trammed background. This can be a desired design feature, and obviously the depth of padding will depend on the thickness of the laid threads. The added advantage of trammed areas, of course, will be a

more hard-wearing needlepoint. This is exactly the reason why so many church kneelers being stitched today use tramming.

- Lastly, as used in Victorian times, the trammed threads help to cover the canvas threads. This is particularly useful for many of the decorative stitches where gaps are unavoidable. It means that a wider choice of threads can be employed without concern over canvas coverage.

Working trammed areas

Canvas

Penelope or double canvas is the usual type for tramming. Mono or interlock canvas is not really suitable, as the tramming threads lie to one side of the stitch, instead of in the centre as when using double canvas (Fig 2.10).

Fig 2.10 Tramming threads on different types of canvas.

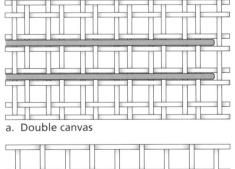

a. Double canvas

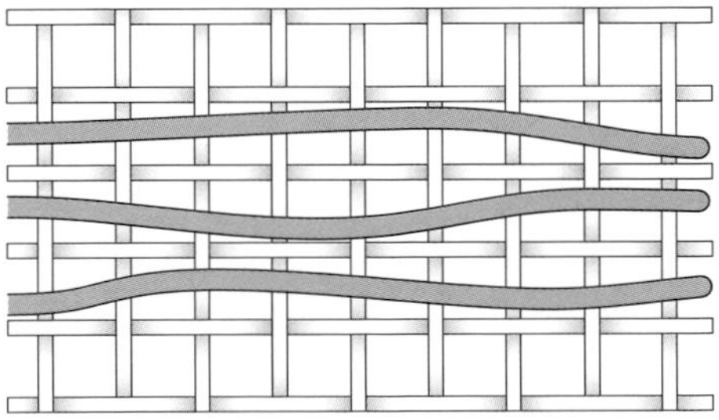

b. Mono/interlock canvas

Threads

Any thread suitable for needlepoint can be used for tramming; however, it is customary to use a thinner version of the yarn to be used for stitching over – for example, one strand of crewel for tramming, with two or three strands of crewel, or one strand of tapestry for overstitching, would be ideal for a 12-gauge canvas. For a more raised effect, use the same thickness of thread for both processes.

Needles

Use a finer needle for the thinner tramming thread than for the main stitching yarn.

Method

1 Place long running stitches across the full width of one colour area, up to a maximum length of 5cm (2in) per stitch.
2 Anchor these lengths with a small back stitch over one canvas thread. Vary the position of these stitches from one line to the next, so that no ridge appears when the overstitching is completed (Fig 2.11). All tramming should be finished before going on to the next step.
3 Stitching over the trammed threads is carried out in the usual way.

Fig 2.11 Arranging the tramming threads to avoid forming ridges.

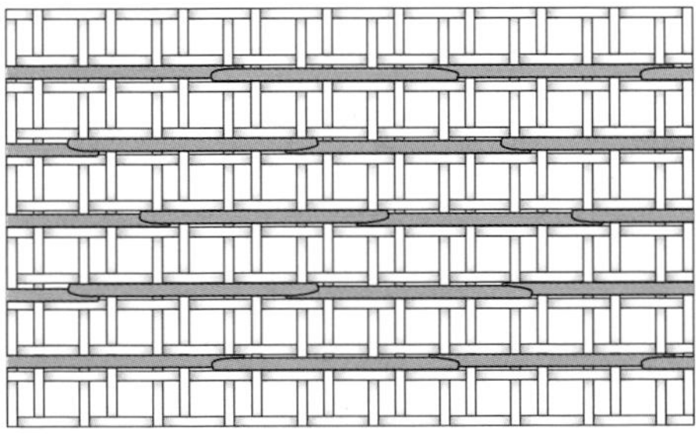

11 Georgian Style Floral Seat Cover

The design for this antique Georgian chair seat has been based on a rather threadbare piece of needlepoint found attached to the chair. This was certainly not as old as the chair itself, as the reverse side revealed the remains of very strong wool colours, probably from the popular Victorian aniline dyes. This design, however, is fairly reminiscent of Georgian needlepoint, as it is a mixture of both exotic and naturalistic flowers and birds. The earlier trend of all-over stylized crewel work with heavy Oriental influences had, by the Georgian era, begun to give way to more centralized sprays of natural flowers: roses, tulips, primulas, and carnations.

The central design area is ideal for the tramming technique, with the background left flat as an additional contrast. Subtle crewel-wool shading of the background has created a rather 'antique' look, very much in keeping with the chair.

This type of seat, which is completely removable from the chair frame, is known as a **drop-in** or **loose** seat. Although they were extremely popular with the designers of the Georgian era, numerous styles have been seen since, especially in the 1930s and 1950s, right up to the present day.

How to stitch

1 Mark the centre of the canvas and extend the lines out to the edge, marking the centre of each side.
2 Attach to a frame and tram all the design using 1 strand of crewel wool in the appropriate colour. If a more raised effect is preferred, then use two strands of wool.
3 Stitch over the tramming using continental tent stitch and two strands of

Finished size:

Central design approximately 39 x 32cm (15½ x 12½in); overall 56 x 48cm (22 x 19in).

You will need

- 11 hpi double canvas, white, 66 x 58cm (26 x 23in)
- Appletons' crewel wool.
  - 1 skein each of 103, 156, 204, 241, 251A, 252, 292, 351, 352, 353, 451, 562, 564, 602, 641, 642, 693, 751, 754, 756, 851, 875, 877, 885, 902, 910
  - 1 hank each of 201, 202
  - 4 hanks 121
- tapestry needle, size 20
- staples and staple gun
- padded drop-in seat, 54 x 46cm (21 x 18in)

wool in the appropriate colour.
4 Complete the background using basketweave stitch, starting in the top right-hand corner, and again using two strands of wool. The main colour is no. 121, with strands of 201 and 202 randomly added.
5 Remove from the frame and attach to the seat frame, referring to pages 131–2.

Adapting the design

There are many possibilities here:

- The background area is very easily changed to fit another chair or stool size.
- The central design is quite suitable for a decorative cushion, either square or round in shape.
- Select your favourite motif or small group of motifs, and use for a suitable-sized project, such as glasses or scissors case, pincushion, needlecase, bookmark, or mirror or picture frame. The thread could be changed to a more decorative one, such as stranded cotton or silk, if appropriate for the project.

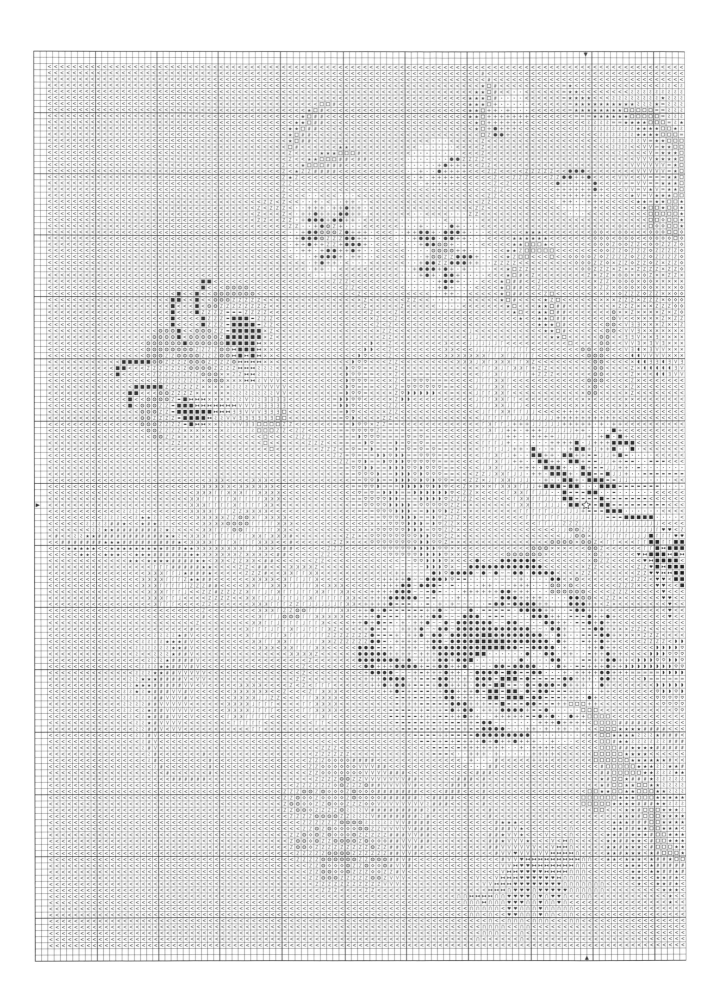

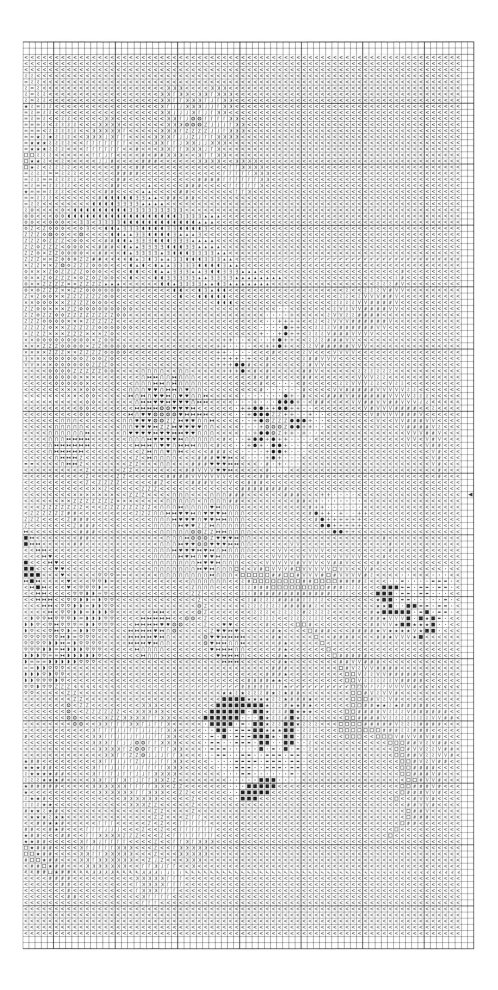

Key

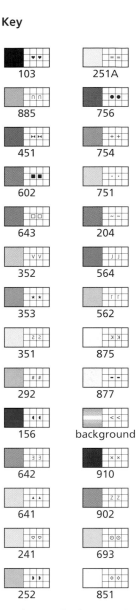

103   251A

885   756

451   754

602   751

643   204

352   564

353   562

351   875

292   877

156   background

642   910

641   902

241   693

252   851

Background colour consists
of 121 with strands of 201
and 202 randomly added

**NB: The chart shows only the
central design area. The plain
background should be
extended to fit the chair or
stool available.**

Beadwork

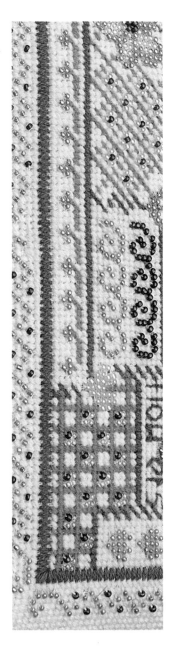

Beadwork on canvas is a straight-forward technique in which each bead is attached over an inter-section of canvas threads. A piece of work may be made up entirely of beads, or the beads may be used as highlighted areas within normal needlepoint stitching. Beads are usually used either for their unique texture or for their shiny, sparkly appearance. It is amazing how heavy a solid panel of beadwork becomes, which, of course, depending on the item, can improve its draping qualities considerably. An important factor to consider when understanding a beadwork project is the time-consuming nature of the technique.

Beads have been used for embroidery in Great Britain since medieval times, when they were imported from Italy, France, and Germany. However, it was in the 19th century that beadwork on canvas became firmly established. Initially, beads were added to the Berlin woolwork as highlights to provide contrasts, but subsequently they became a totally independent and very popular technique. Readily available beadwork pattern-books included instructions for interior furnishing items such as cushions, furniture, firescreens, and tea cosies, as well as personal accessories such as slippers, spectacle cases, bags, and purses.

A great variety of beads were available: small tubular ones called 'bugles', round seed beads from coloured glass, and more decorative beads cut from steel, gold, silver, coral, and pearls. Waxed thread, chosen for its strength and durability, was used for attaching the beads. Despite this, it is interesting to note that on many pieces of antique needlepoint with beaded areas, it is the threads attaching the beads which have worn the most, resulting in a loss of beads. Early this century, beadwork moved away from being used for canvas work and became associated with the fashion scene. However, along with so many other needlwork techniques, beadwork, after many long years of mediocre interest, is enjoying a revival.

Stitching beadwork

Canvas

It is very important to match the gauge of the canvas to the bead size being used. If the canvas gauge is too small the beads will not fit smoothly and will tend to buckle and bulge, giving a very ragged general appearance. Conversely, if the gauge is too large, gaps of canvas will be visible between the beads. For the widely available seed beads, as used in the sewing-box project in this chapter, a 13 hpi canvas is a perfect size. A double or Penelope canvas is preferable to an interlock one, as it provides a two-line grid for the beads to sit on. A de luxe polished mono canvas is not advisable, as the beads have to perch on top of the threads, and more often will slip down to one side or the other.

Threads

Traditionally, beads have been attached to the canvas with double waxed silk thread. However, the modern alternative is strong double polyester sewing thread, although a strong cotton thread rubbed with beeswax can still be used if preferred. Try to use a fairly neutral colour such as cream, beige, or grey if a number of different colours of beads are being stitched; otherwise, match the thread as closely as possible to the bead colour.

Needles

Use special beading needles, which are long and thin with a sharp point and should fit easily through the bead centres. Use a needle threader, as the eyes of these needles are very fine.

Method

Always work whole rows of beads – not areas of one colour as for needlepoint – beginning at the top and working in rows downwards. Complete all beadwork before any stitching is started in thread or yarn. It is often recommended that beads are attached with the same stitch as any surrounding needlepoint; however, half-cross and continental tent stitch will be the only contenders here. Of the two, the continental is preferable as it tends to hold the bead in place more firmly (see Fig 2.12).

Fig 2.12 Attaching beads.

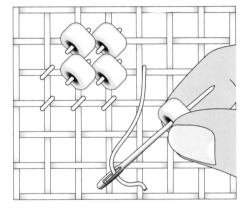

12 Hearts and Flowers Sewing Box Lid

The traditional technique of beading has been used for this contemporary bordered design. The several shades of blue and green beads contrast sharply with the array of stitched patterns and the additional surface stitching used to create the writing. Additional interest has been achieved by using varying combinations of ecru and white threads for the background areas.

Finished size

12.5 x 26.5cm (5½ x 10½in)

How to stitch

1 Attach to a frame in the usual way, having first marked the centre of the canvas.

2 All stitching is in continental tent stitch except for the dark blue border. This is worked in straight stitch over two canvas threads, over two tramming threads (see Fig 2.13).

Fig 2.13 Stitching the trammed border.

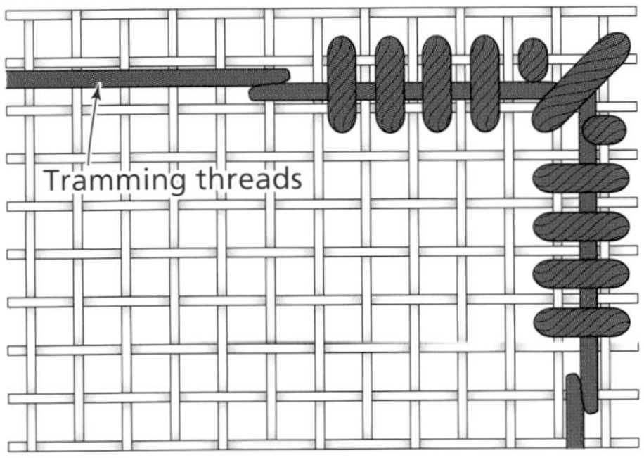

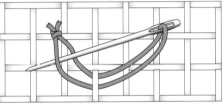

3 Three strands of wool are used throughout, except for the writing over the tent stitching, which uses only two strands.

4 Start by stitching all the dividing lines, including the dark blue border.

5 Next, attach all the beads using double cotton and the beading needle. Use a knot a short distance away to start, but catch the thread through the

You will need

- 12 hpi double canvas, white, 22.5 x 36.5cm (7 x 12½in)
- DMC seed beads:
  - 1 pkt. each of 794S, 813S, 828S, 3811S
  - 2 pkts. 931A
  - 3 pkts. 959S
- DMC Broder Medicis crewel wool:

- 1 skein each of 8930, 8997
- 3 skeins blanc
- 4 skeins ecru
- beige polyester sewing thread
- beading needle
- tapestry needle, size 20
- sewing box with a 12.5 x 26.5cm (5 x 10½in) cushion pad

Fig 2.14 Starting a beading thread.

Wrong side of canvas

knot for extra security (Fig 2.14).

6 Select the right combination of wool colours to fill in the various background areas, once the patterns are all complete.

7 Finish this middle section by backstitching the writing 'Hearts and Flowers'.

8 For the outer border, attach the beads first, then fill in the background.

9 Remove from the frame and refer to page 132 for attaching to the box lid.

For best results

- Keep the thread as tight as possible when attaching the beads, so they are firmly held on the canvas.
- Discard any particularly large or misshapen beads to achieve uniform lines.

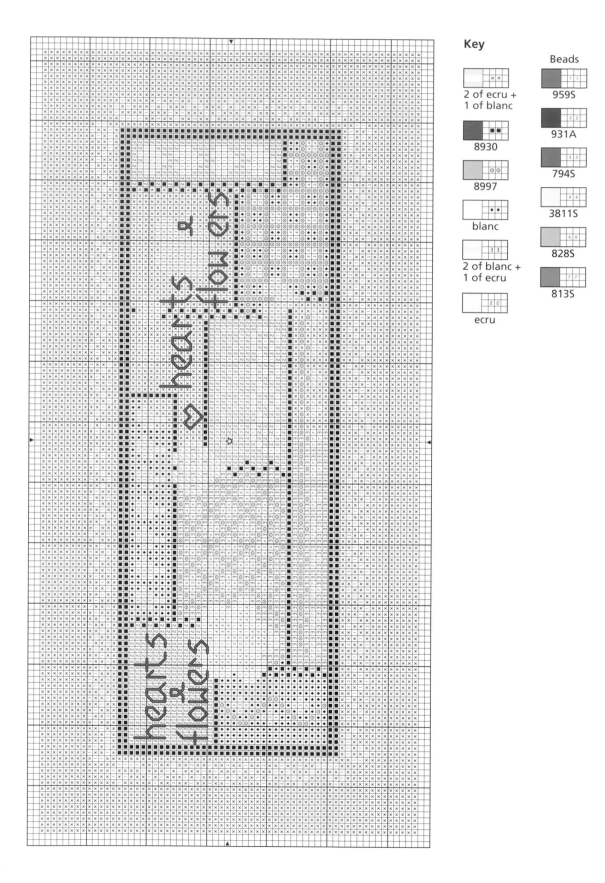

Key

2 of ecru +
1 of blanc

8930

8997

blanc

2 of blanc +
1 of ecru

ecru

Beads

959S

931A

794S

3811S

828S

813S

Waste Canvas

Waste canvas – or **tear-away** canvas, **waste fabric**, or **blue line** canvas as it is sometimes known – looks just like other double-thread canvases. However, it has one distinguishing feature: blue lines running vertically, occurring every five pairs of threads. It is designed to be a temporary, disposable canvas, that is used to aid stitching on a non-evenweave fabric – that is, one where the warp and weft threads are of different thicknesses – or a non-woven fabric such as felt. Once stitching is completed, the starch-coated canvas threads are dampened to dissolve the starch, which makes for easy removal of the threads. The chief advantage of this product is that any cross-stitch or needlepoint charts and patterns can be used on a non-evenweave fabric, and the patterns can be placed at any angle, irrespective of the fabric weave. The other important advantage is that by including a ready-made fabric as a

background to the design, all background stitching is eliminated.

This technique of removing canvas from fabric after stitching seems to have been used as early as the 18th century and intermittently since. Many old needlework books describe the technique, recommending an even-weave linen as a suitable waste canvas. The actual blue-line canvas was first manufactured in 1976, but mono canvas or linen can still be used instead.

Stitching waste canvas

Canvas

Mesh sizes range from 8/9 to 14 hpi in one width of 68cm (27in), although a 16 hpi version is available in the United States. Background fabrics such as those with a pile, or relatively thick ones such as felt, are particularly suitable, as the

Threads for Waste Canvas

Waste canvas hpi	Recommended number of strands					
	Stranded cotton		Tapestry wool		Crewel wool	
	Cross stitch	Straight stitch	Cross stitch	Straight stitch	Cross stitch	Straight stitch
8–9	6	–	1	2	3	6
10	4	–	2	3	3	5
12	3	–	–	1	2	4
14	2	6	–	1	1	3

stitches can sink into them once the canvas is removed. This is particularly important if beads are being incorporated into the design – otherwise they will wobble and look irregular. Very thin fabrics and sheers do not always produce a satisfactory result unless a thin padding of polyester wadding is included.

Threads

A variety of yarns may be used, the thickness of which should match the canvas mesh size and the stitch to be used (see the table below).

Needles

Depending on the chosen backing fabric, a sharp-pointed needle may be preferred to a blunt-ended tapestry needle. Choose the appropriate size for the canvas gauge and thread selected. Care should be taken if using a sharp needle not to pierce the canvas threads.

Stitches

Any needlepoint stitches can be used; however, if the design has many isolated stitches and rows of stitches, rather than solid blocks, then 'complete' stitches such as cross stitch create a better finished

appearance than a one-directional stitch such as tent or basketweave.

Method

The canvas should be tacked into place on the fabric. Stitches radiating out from the centre as well as around the edges ensure that the canvas is held securely (Fig 2.15). The usual method of stitching is over pairs of threads, and these stitches can be placed in two different ways: firstly, with the needle and thread using the large holes (Fig 2.16a); secondly, with needle and thread using the smaller holes (Fig 2.16b).

Fig 2.16 Stitching waste canvas.

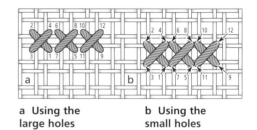

a Using the large holes   **b Using the small holes**

The latter method has the advantage that the stitches are positioned and held in place more accurately; however, if the smaller-gauge canvases are used the holes become too small to accommodate more than one stitch. Alternatively, the waste canvas can be used as a double canvas, creating petit-point-size stitching. However, over large areas of this it would be extremely difficult to remove the canvas threads on completion.

All stitching should be worked slightly tighter than normal, as the tension will slacken once the waste canvas is removed. Use the **stab stitch** method, where the thread is pulled through completely to the wrong side before coming back through to the right side. A frame is not essential unless large areas of tent stitch are to be worked, although it would save the backing fabric from constant handling. If

Fig 2.15 Attaching waste canvas.

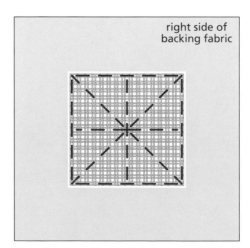

one is used, then attach it to the backing fabric well beyond the area that will eventually be the finished article. On reasonably large projects, such as the animal cushion, start stitching from the centre outwards, as this will avoid any puckering of the fabric underneath.

Once stitching is completed, cut away any unused canvas to within 2cm (¾in). The canvas can now be dampened with a fine water spray. Once the threads have softened, they should be removed one at a time, to minimize disturbance of the stitching. Tweezers can be helpful if any of the threads seem particularly stubborn. If dampening is not advisable because of the yarn or fabric used, then crumple the canvas to break up the starch coating before trying to remove it.

13 Animal Cushion

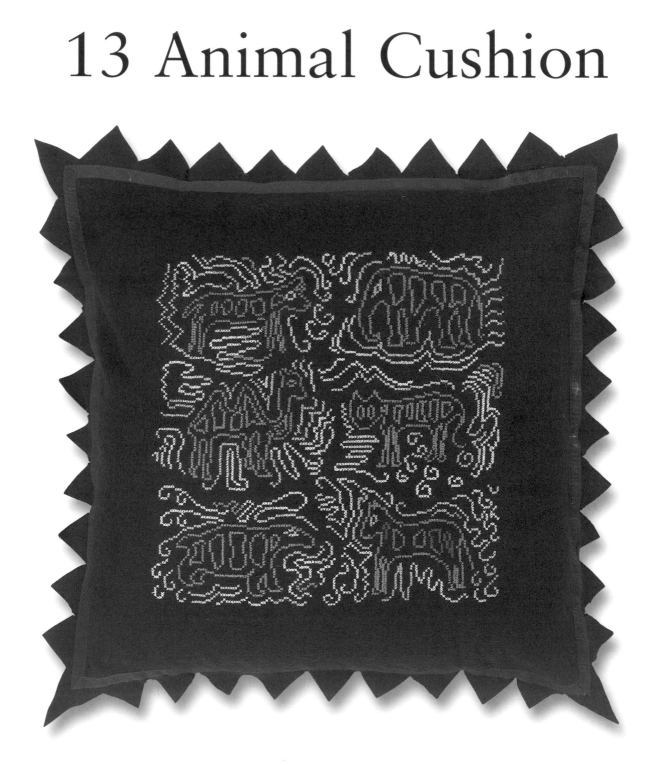

This delightful project was inspired by the present popular interest in wildlife. The animal panels are quite independent, so a favourite one could easily stand alone on a smaller project.

Finished size

41cm (16in) square

How to stitch

1 Attach the waste canvas to the piece of felt, using large tacking stitches.
2 Using two strands of cotton at all times, start working on the outline of one of the centre animals. Complete the other outline before filling in, and then stitch the lines around them.
3 Move on to the top pair of animals, and then the bottom two, working in the same order.
4 Cut away excess canvas; dampen the remaining canvas slightly (see 'For Best Results'), then remove the threads carefully.
5 Refer to page 132 for finishing instructions.

For best results

- Test the base fabric and threads used for colour fastness, before spraying with water.
- When cutting the excess waste canvas, do not cut right up to the stitching, as you will need the 2cm (¾in) to hold on to in order to pull the threads out.

You will need

- 14 hpi waste canvas, 33 x 36cm (13 x 14¼in)
- DMC stranded cotton. 1 skein each of 209, 211, 3814, 743, 745, 747, 825, 959, 3755, 3761
- navy felt, 50cm (19¾in) square
- matching sewing thread
- 36cm (14in) navy zip
- feather cushion pad, 41cm (16in) square
- 1.8m (5ft) of 1cm-wide blue ribbon
- piece of fabric for the back of the cushion, 49cm (19in) square

- When removing the threads, try to take out the warp threads first, as these are generally slightly stronger and may pull out without breaking. (The warp threads are the vertical threads, parallel to the blue lines.)
- Take great care with this process so as not to damage the stitching or fabric underneath.

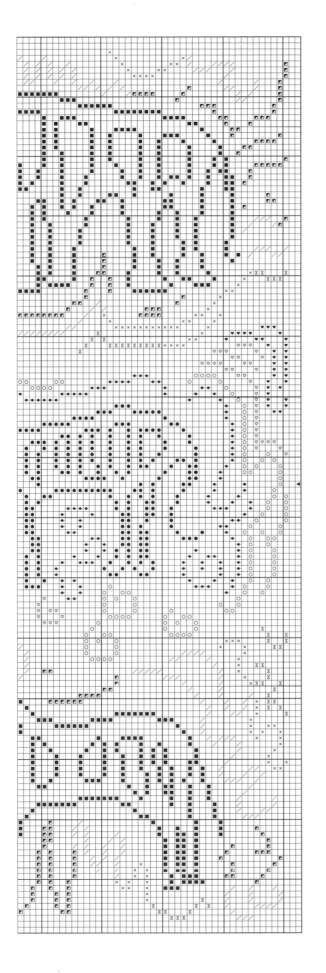

Key

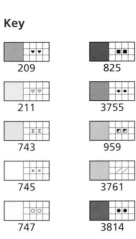

209

211

743

745

747

825

3755

959

3761

3814

Part Three
Variation and
Experimentation

Experimenting with Colour and Texture

In recent years, with the tremendous surge of interest in all needlecrafts, there has not only been a revival of traditional techniques and skills, but a committed pursuit of new ideas by experimenting and adapting. In the needlepoint field every element – colour, design, threads, techniques, canvas, and stitches – has been explored and developed. Increasingly, also, needlepoint is being used for a wider range of furnishings and personal items – really as many as in Victorian times when canvas work was in its heyday.

Threads

The traditionally used tapestry and crewel wools continue to increase in their colour ranges, with new shades being added to them all the time. However, the real explosion in threads has been in those for more decorative purposes – perle, stranded and soft cottons, linen, silk, rayon/viscose, metallic (including glitter yarn), synthetics and mixtures, textured bouclés, twists, and chenilles. Specialist wools are available from particular breeds of sheep, as well as wool combined with other animal hair, such as cat, dog, rabbit, and soft-haired zoo animals. Natural dyes are increasingly being used, especially for wools, with colours from vegetables, fruits, leaves, ferns, and flowers such as camomile, heather, indigo, and madder. There is now also an enormous variety of shaded threads available commercially, which can all be used for needlepoint by varying the number of strands in the needle.

The following two needlecases employ a combination of both modern and traditional elements. A different type of shaded thread has been used for each side, together with a different quilting design. These traditional quilting patterns, such as twisted and feathered borders, flowers, circles, knots, hearts, and spirals were all in use as early as the 12th century, for knights' and crusaders' padded garments.

14 Two Needlecases
in Quilting Patterns

Finished size

10.5cm (4¼in) square.

Method for both designs

1 A frame is optional, but you may find it an advantage to use one so as not to crumple stitching already worked.

2 Use the following number of strands in the needle at a time:

- DMC stranded cotton: 3 strands
- Caron silk/wool: 1 strand
- De Haviland rayon: 3 strands
- Colinette silk: 1 strand
- Coats' Bond Multi: 1 strand.

3 Stitch the design first using the white stranded cotton, then fill in around this with the variegated thread, using continental tent stitch.

4 Make up according to the instructions for Project 1 on page 122.

You will need

- 17 hpi mono or interlock canvas, 20.5 x 31cm (8 x 12in)
- Needlecase No 1:
  - Side 1: Caron 'Impressions', 50% silk/50% wool, 2 skeins Mediterranean
  - Side 2: De Haviland Imitation silk, 100% rayon, 1 skein blue/ green

- Needlecase No 2:
  - Side 1: Colinette Yarn 100% silk, 2 skeins Nauticus
  - Side 2: Coats' Bond Multi cotton/rayon/nylon, 1 reel blue/ green
- 2 skeins DMC stranded cotton, blanc
- tapestry needle, size 22

- piece of interlining or wadding, 10.5 x 21cm (8¼ x 16½in)
- piece of lining fabric in a matching colour, 13.5 x 24cm (5¼ x 9½in)
- piece of felt in a matching colour, 19 x 17cm (7½ x 6¾in)
- matching sewing thread

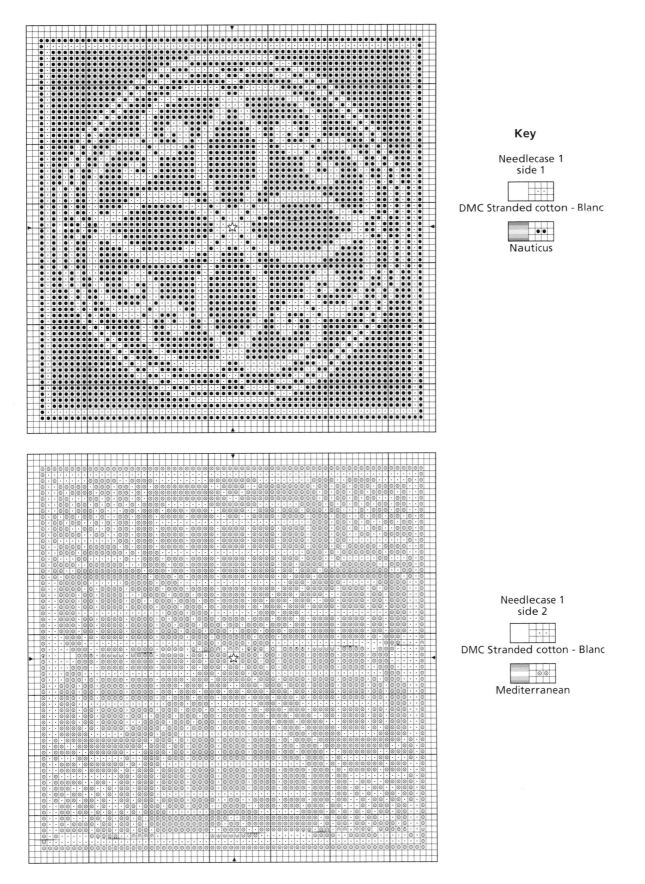

Key

Needlecase 1
side 1

DMC Stranded cotton - Blanc

Nauticus

Needlecase 1
side 2

DMC Stranded cotton - Blanc

Mediterranean

Key

Needlecase 2
side 1

DMC Stranded cotton - Blanc

Blue/green

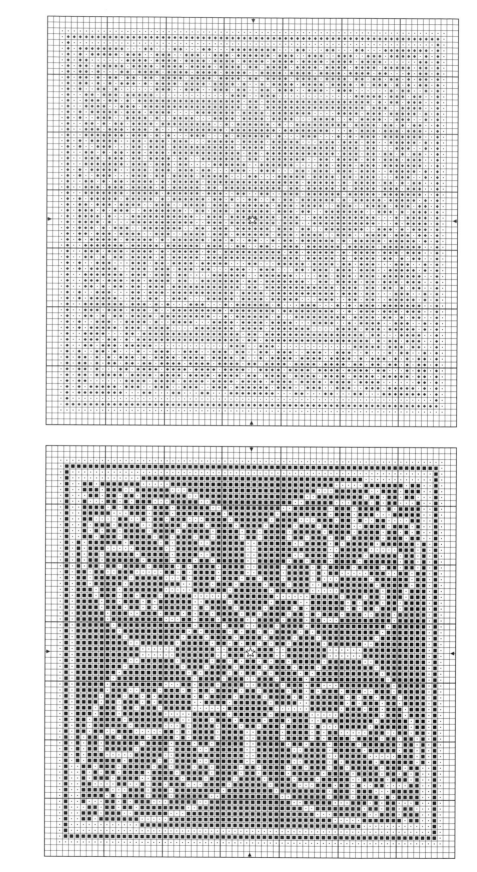

Needlecase 2
side 2

DMC Stranded cotton - Blanc

Blue/green

Space Dyeing

Dyeing yarn yourself to achieve a shaded effect – space dyeing – is a very easy way to produce a totally original thread, with the added advantage of allowing you to choose exact colour combinations. Any yarn may be used, but care must be taken to select the right type of dye, as some are specifically designed for either natural or synthetic fibres only. The Dylon cold-water dyes used in the following cushion project are recommended for silk, wool, linen, cotton, and viscose, but not for synthetics or fabrics with special finishes. The most difficult part of space-dyeing is trying to reproduce a second time the exact colours of a previous dyeing.

Method

1 Make up the following solutions using glass jam-jars (measurements are approximate):

- salt solution: 50g (2oz) salt dissolved in 0.25 litre (½pt) hot water
- soda solution: 14g (½oz) washing soda dissolved in 100ml (4 fl oz) hot water, then diluted in 1 litre (2pt) water
- dye solutions: ½tsp of dye powder dissolved in tablespoon of the salt solution, then diluted by half-filling the jar with hot water. Make up a separate dye solution for each colour to be used.

2 The yarn to be used should be in small hanks of approximately 5–10m (5–10yds) and tied with a loose thread to prevent it unwinding and becoming tangled. Soak these in water first and squeeze out any excess.

3 Lay the hanks in a single layer on a tray or in a shallow dish and spoon over each dye in turn, ensuring an overlapping and merging of colours. Leave in the dye for approximately 15 minutes to ensure that the colours have been thoroughly absorbed.

4 To fix the colours of the dyes, carefully pour over the soda solution and leave for 30 minutes.

5 Rinse the yarn, then wash gently in warm soapy water, rinse again, then dry.

For best results

- Always experiment beforehand with the dyes and thread to ensure that the final colours are acceptable.
- Remember that when dry, the threads will be paler than in the dye water.
- When the threads are soaking in the soda solution, do not stir, as this mixes up the colours and can cause brown marks to appear.

15 Space-Dyed Cushion

This project continues with the traditional quilting patterns, but using your own space-dyed yarn. The dye mixtures were initially tried on both wool and cotton threads, with the cotton being chosen as it absorbed the colours more effectively.

Finished size

41cm (16in) square

Method

1 Dye 30 skeins of cotton following the instructions given on page 93. Try to con-centrate the colours in these proportions:

- mainly blue – 8 skeins
- mainly green – 15 skeins
- mainly pale – 7 skeins

2 For the pale skeins, use the dyes watered down to half strength.

3 Dry thoroughly and check that the thread is tangle- and knot-free.

4 Frame the canvas and stitch in half-cross stitch throughout with 1 strand of cotton. Work the white lines first, then stitch complete rows for each colour shade.

5 Remove from the frame and refer to the instructions on pages 132–3.

Key

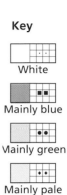

White

Mainly blue

Mainly green

Mainly pale

You will need

- 12 hpi white interlock canvas, 51cm (20in) square
- DMC soft cotton, 40 skeins white
- tapestry needle, size 18
- Dylon cold-water dyes:
  - light blue, no. 6
  - lavender, no. 17
- royal blue, no. 26
- turquoise, no. 53
- green, no. 59
- dyeing equipment as described above
- matching plain fabric: 0.5m (20in) turquoise/blue
- matching sewing thread
- decorative cord: 1.8m (5ft) blue/green mix
- small tassels: 12, to match cord
- feather cushion pad, 41cm (16in) square

Tie-Dyeing

Another method of dyeing threads using these cold-water dyes is by tie-dyeing. There are several different ways of tying the yarn, but all with the same effect of leaving the tied areas un-dyed (Fig 3.1). Use small skeins, or cut the yarn into manageable lengths before tying.

Fig 3.1 Methods of tying the yarn for tie-dyeing.

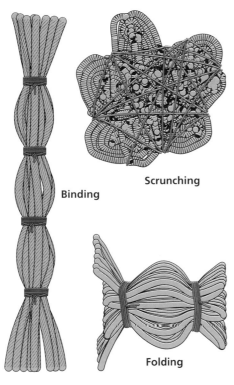

Binding

Scrunching

Folding

Method

1 Prepare the dyes as before, using one or more colours.

2 Prepare the yarn by scrunching or folding, then binding with string; immerse into the dyes.

3 Remove from the dye and allow the yarn to dry completely before untying the string. Fig 3.2 shows the desired result.

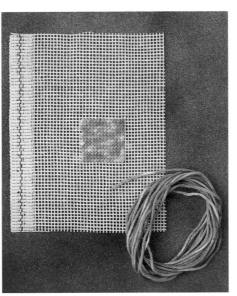

Fig 3.2 Tie-dyed yarn.

For best results

- Colours will intensify the longer the threads are left immersed in the dye.
- The string must be tied as tightly as possible or the dye will seep underneath.

Using fabric paints

Finally, an alternative method of colouring threads is by using fabric paints. Yarn can be wound onto card, and then painted with a brush in vertical, horizontal, or random stripes (see Fig 3.3). 'Colourfun' by Dylon or DEKA silk paints would be suitable for this, but would need to be heat-set by light ironing afterwards. The main advantage of this method is that you have complete control over the amount and position of the colours. However, as with all variable coloured threads, the effect when stitched is still an unknown quantity (see Fig 3.4).

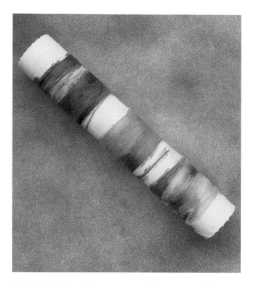

Fig 3.3 Painted yarn wound onto card.

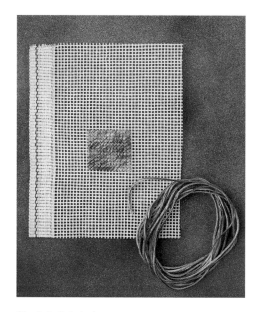

Fig 3.4 Painted yarn.

Canvas

Experimentation with canvas has been taking several different directions. Colouring has been achieved by sponging, dyeing, spray-painting, stencilling, and marbling, usually with the intention of leaving parts unstitched as a feature.

Stitching on canvas has been equally diverse, with both close and spaced zigzag stitching, couching (applying threads and ribbons to the surface), and canvas motifs appliquéd onto a different gauge canvas or other material. Recently, there has been the use of hessian or similar as a substitute for canvas. Here the slight irregularities of the warp and weft threads make the stitching in turn similarly uneven; this then becomes a feature instead of an indication of poor stitching.

Designing Needlepoint

Once you have mastered the basic stitches and tried the advanced techniques, you may feel that designing your own work is the next logical step. The obvious advantage is that you have complete control over the actual design: its size, shape, content, colours, stitches, and threads. This means that it can be tailor-made to fit a particular item such as a chair seat, can co-ordinate exactly with existing decor features within a room, or can depict some much-loved item or idea. In addition, it can be a really exciting and satisfying experience to actually create and stitch your own original design.

The design process can be split into the following easy steps:

Step 1

Decide on the project, and make a paper template to the size required. Rugs and carpets, cushions and cushion panels, tie-backs and chair coverings, book covers and picture frames, are all suitable items, as well as the great variety of boxes, screens, cupboards, frames, and stools which are now specifically made to accommodate stitched panels.

Step 2

Decide on the actual design. This can be based on existing finishings in a room – fabric, wallpaper, tiles, carpets, and rugs – or on a favourite artefact, piece of china, picture, chair covering, or whatever. Other man-made sources of inspiration include stone carving, ironwork, machinery, books, paintings, decorative glassware, silver and brass ware, and mosaics. Museums, art galleries, exhibitions, libraries, and stately homes can provide an infinite source of ideas. Alternatively, natural sources may be used, such as flowers, leaves, plants, trees, land- and seascapes, fossils, shells, minerals and rock formations, birds, animals, fish, and insects. Try to be visually aware of all potential sources for design, including the less obvious ones such as oil patches in puddles, a squashed drinks can, graffiti,

a pile of logs, and so on. Ideally the design should be drawn from the source itself; if this is not possible, use photographs, pictures, and photocopies.

It is important to look at the source closely, to see the real shape, the proportions, the lines and the colours, as drawing from memory often produces a second-rate result. A notebook can be invaluable here for recording ideas and sketching details, as well as a scrapbook of pictures and magazine cuttings to provide inspiration at a later date.

For more detailed observations try using a magnifying glass; you will be pleasantly surprised by the intricate details not normally visible. For more abstract effects, suitable methods of recording or creating a design would be rubbings, doodles, folded and cut paper, torn paper, collage, ink blots, paint bubbles, lines of wiggly string, and exploded pictures. An exploded picture is a design cut up into pieces, using straight or curved cuts to produce randomly sized shapes, then put back together to make a different pattern (Fig 3.5).

A **viewer** or **finder**, which is a piece of paper with a shaped aperture cut out of it, can sometimes help to isolate an area of a picture, drawing, or pattern, which can then be developed into the final design. An adjustable viewer can easily be made from two L-shaped pieces of card, which are overlapped to produce a rectangular opening of variable size.

The actual style of the design needs also to be considered here. It could be

- **realistic**, resembling the source as nearly as possible;
- **stylized**, where the source is still recognizable, but certain elements have been emphasized to the

Fig 3.5 Stages in making an exploded picture.

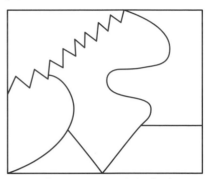

a **The picture as originally drawn.**

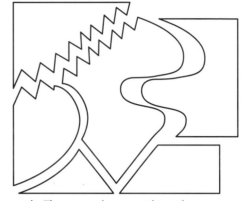

b **The same picture cut into pieces.**

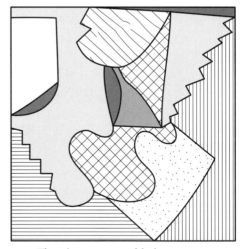

c **The pieces reassembled.**

detriment of others (this usually involves a conscious effort to simplify the source material); or
- **abstract** – either an abstraction of the original source, so that it is no longer recognizable (as can be seen in the last of the series of whale

patterns later in this chapter), or based on an abstract source, which might include geometric shapes.

Step 3

Make a design on your paper template, which can be centralized, randomly placed, bordered, repeated, or staggered. To help with the positioning of a repeat motif the area can be overlaid with a regularly spaced grid or divided into sections – squares, rectangles, diamonds, hexagons, triangles, circles, or strips. This grid can then be retained to form part of the overall design, giving a rather formal effect (as can be seen in the Maple Leaf Cushion Panel, Project 6), or removed if less formality is preferred. Informality could also be achieved by using a more irregular grid such as intersecting wavy lines. Non-uniform grids, such as squares of diminishing size, can create an impression of depth and distance.

It can be useful at this stage to cut out paper patterns of the motifs in their correct sizes. These can then be arranged until you are satisfied with the result, and a successful composition is achieved. This process will quickly answer questions such as 'How do I know if the pattern will work?', or 'Will it achieve the effect I want?' Stitching a sample large enough to enable you to visualize the end result would be far too time-consuming. This paper-shape method was used when designing both the Tropical Leaf needlepoint arrangement (Project 7) and the stencilled fabric surrounding it.

It may be that the motif already drawn is required in a different size. Photocopiers are ideal for both enlarging and reducing. However, in the absence of one of these, use the

following paper-and-pencil method.

1 Enclose the motif with a square or rectangle and divide this up into squares (see Fig 3.6a).

2 Draw a new square or rectangle to the required size, and to the same proportions as the first rectangle; divide it up into the same number of squares as before.

Fig 3.6 Enlarging and distorting a motif.

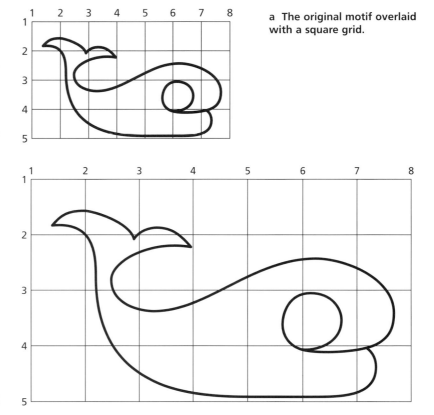

a The original motif overlaid with a square grid.

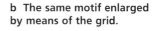

b The same motif enlarged by means of the grid.

3 Carefully draw in the motif free-hand, using the grid as a guide (see Fig 3.6b). If a distorted version of the motif is required, this can be easily done by extending the square or rectangle in one direction only (see Fig 3.6c–d). Sometimes the shape of a motif must be changed to fit into a particular space, such as a hexagon or triangle. The easiest way to achieve this is to draw the motif on a piece of thin stretchy fabric and pull the fabric in the places where it

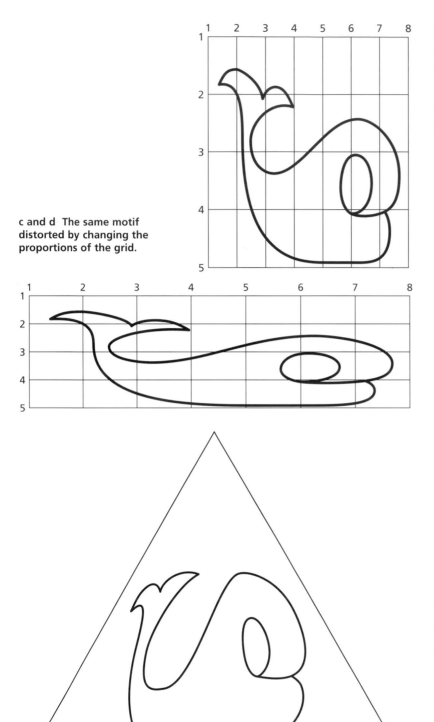

c and d The same motif distorted by changing the proportions of the grid.

e The same motif distorted by stretching the fabric.

is to be extended (see Fig 3.6e). Great fun can be had by deliberately distorting a shape into a more amusing form!

Step 4
Ask yourself the following questions:

- Is the size of the design in proportion to the total area to be stitched?
- Does it fill the space available?
- Is there too little or too much background?
- Is it too near the edges of the template?
- Is it suitable for its purpose? For example, a footstool will be viewed from all directions, whereas a chair seat can have a design with a definite 'right way round'.
- Does it have a focal point? It is important for a design to have a focal point, but this does not necessarily have to be placed centrally. It can often create greater interest if it is placed off-centre, as with the tropical leaves in Project 7. However, care must be taken with an asymmetrical design that it does not appear unbalanced.

Step 5
When you are completely satisfied with the design, consider the following elements:

- **Threads** Take into account not only the finished effect desired, but also the function and durability required of the item to be stitched. If the design would benefit from detailed shading, then a divisible or fine thread will be necessary, such as stranded cotton or crewel wool. If decorative stitches are to be used, again a thread that can be varied in thickness may be needed.

- **Canvas** This should be considered in conjunction with the thread chosen and the number of strands needed to cover various canvas gauges. The amount of detail which has been drawn into the design will also help determine the correct gauge; this should be weighed against the extra time involved in stitching fine canvases. It is also useful to consider at this point the general limitations imposed on any design by the geometric nature of the canvas grid. Firstly, once a canvas gauge is selected, a definite number of stitches has to be worked. The only way of varying this number is to work petit-point areas on a double canvas, or to use larger decorative stitches which cover more than one grid intersection at a time, as with rug motifs. Secondly, all curved shapes will have to have a 'stepped' edge, irrespective of the canvas used. This will look just too angular unless a sufficiently small gauge is selected. Slanting lines will also have to be 'stepped', unless they are placed at a 45° angle. Finally, the uniform nature of the holes and intersections means that to cover the canvas a consistent thickness of yarn must be used. A variety of threads can be introduced, however, by combining several strands of thinner ones to make up the required thickness. Working some areas in decorative stitches also gives an opportunity for thinner and thicker threads to be utilized.
- **Stitches** Consider the following points when choosing which stitch or stitches to use:
  - coverage of the canvas, and

whether it is desirable to have a padded wrong side;
- distortion of the canvas;
- the amount of yarn to be used;
- the 'look' and patterns of the stitches;
- their suitability for the design;
- personal preference; and
- speed of stitching.

Step 6

Now it is time to choose colours. Remember always to select these in natural daylight and not by artificial light, and preferably in the room where the item will be finally positioned, as the amount and quality of light varies so much from room to room. The accurate colour charts available for all the well-known thread manufacturers are ideal for this purpose.

Nearly all of us have a subconscious sense of colour composition – that is, the art of combining several colours together. This is seen in the clothes we wear and in the decoration of our homes. However, it can be helpful when selecting a colour scheme to look at the basic colour theory to understand why we choose the colours we do:

- blue and grey: cool effect;
- green: restful;
- yellow: bright and cheerful;
- orange and red: lively and exciting.

Harmonious colours are those which lie next to one another on the colour wheel (see Fig 3.7) and, because they are related, produce an 'easy to look at' effect. Complementary colours – those which are opposite to one another on the colour wheel, such as orange and blue, yellow and purple, red (or pink) and green – produce a contrasting effect. Adding a

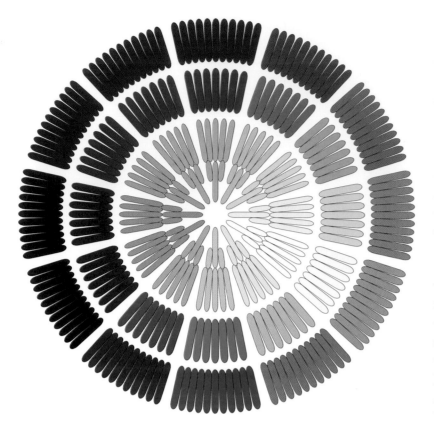

Fig 3.7 The colour wheel. The inner ring shows the *tints*, in which white is added to the basic colours. The next ring shows the basic colours by themselves. The outer ring shows the *shades*, in which black is added to the basic colours.

small amount of a complementary colour to a monochromatic scheme (one which consists of varying shades of one colour) tends to add a touch of excitement. It is interesting to see how some of these colour schemes work in practice, by comparing, say, the harmonious blues and greens of the Space-Dyed Cushion (Project 15) with the complementary reds and greens of the Maple Leaves (Project 6).

Fig 3.8 The colours of a daffodil (above) and a sunset (below).

If you cannot decide on a colour scheme, natural objects may supply you with a ready-made one, and you will be pleasantly surprised at the colours that combine perfectly. Flowers, leaves, fruit and vegetables, shells, bark, and minerals are ideal for this purpose. The upper sample in Fig 3.8 shows wrapped threads in the colour range from a daffodil, and in approximately the same proportions of colours. The lower one has been compiled from a very colourful sunset.

Try using your paper shapes again, but this time using coloured papers, for the background colours as well as the motifs. It is important to view colours in their correct context, as the colours that surround them have a strengthening or weakening effect. A light colour always looks lighter on a dark background, and a dark colour darker against a light background. In addition, light to medium shades will take on colour influences from strongly coloured surrounding areas.

A balance is also needed in colour choices. If all the colours are of equal strength they will all demand equal attention, giving a uniform and relaxing effect. However, when one colour becomes much stronger than the others this will claim greater attention, which tends to produce a much livelier and more exciting result. Obviously, care must be taken not to use such a dominant colour in a background area as to detract attention from the main design. If several strong colours are used at one time, the design becomes very demanding to look at and may even create a sense of chaos.

When choosing the actual colours from the sample cards, remember that the colour you see in one strand of thread will look very much brighter and more intense when stitched in a large area. Also, some of the shades of a colour are only very slightly different and when stitched next to one another, hardly any difference will be visible between them.

Step 7

It is now time to try out all the elements you have selected – canvas, stitches, and colours, as well as shapes, outlines, and shadings – by stitching small samples. This will determine whether they all work together, to produce the desired result.

Step 8

Calculate the amount of yarn needed by stitching a 2.5cm (1in) square on canvas of the chosen gauge. It is better to over-estimate quantities slightly than to run short, as different dye lots can vary slightly.

Step 9

Transferring the design onto the canvas is the final stage. There are various methods of doing this.

- The design can be drawn on paper and the canvas placed over it. If the outlines are coloured over in a thick felt-tip pen, then it will be easy to see them through the canvas. Secure the canvas to the paper with paper-clips and use a permanent marker pen, in an appropriate colour for the threads you will be using (see Fig 3.9). Alternatively, the outlines can be painted with a fine brush and acrylic paint. Once the design is on the canvas, areas can be painted in using thin acrylic paint. This method is suitable for pictorial designs, but not for repeat patterns, where greater accuracy is needed.

Fig 3.9 Tracing a motif onto canvas.

Fig 3.10 Motif drawn in fabric paints and ironed onto the canvas.

An interesting alternative is the use of fabric transfers, paints, or crayons. These are used on paper first, where the design can be altered and changed until perfect, before ironing it onto the canvas (see Fig 3.10). The crayons are more restrictive to use than the paints – the mixing of colours is far less easy to achieve.

- Graphed tracing paper can be placed over the drawn design. This is readily available in most canvas sizes, and is very useful where certain areas, such as those containing detailed shading, need to be worked out in full before stitching. Tracing on graphed paper can also be used effectively to reduce or enlarge a design. For example, if the original design is 6in (15cm) square, using a 14 hpi grid paper will give 14 x 6 = 84 squares. Stitched on a 12 hpi canvas this will give a finished size of 84/12 = 7in (18cm) square. Using a 10 hpi grid paper will give 10 x 6 = 60 squares; stitched on a 12 hpi canvas, the finished size will be 60/12 = 5in (12.5cm) square. Alternatively, a photocopier can reduce or enlarge the original drawing to the correct stitching size.

- The drawing may be made on normal graph paper in the first place, so that the squares can then be coloured in as necessary. This is useful for working out repeat patterns, but the graph paper must be the same grid size as the canvas to be stitched on.

Backgrounds

One element which is often ignored in the designing process is the background area. This is usually stitched in a solid and sometimes rather uninteresting colour, which would seem to be a missed opportunity for adding an extra dimension to the whole project. Admittedly a background usually needs to be unobtrusive so that it is not competing with the main design; however, there is still scope to make it interesting.

As we saw on pages 44–5 (Crewel Wool Shading), the mixing of shades and colours is ideal for backgrounds – both overall mixing, as for the Repeat-Patterned Glasses Case, Maple Leaf Cushion, and Georgian-Style Seat Cover (Projects 3, 6, and 11), as well as the randomly placed additional colours seen in the Flower and Fish Chair Seat, Tropical Leaf Cushion and Ship Seat Cover (Projects 2, 7, and 17).

Alternatively, a variety of small patterns can be stitched in slightly varying colours. Checks and tartans can be effectively used as can be seen in the background to the Ship design (Project 17). Try making up your own simple check by using just two colours; if you want a third, use alternate stitches of the first two colours, or use crewel wool and mix the colours

in the needle. For a background design based on curving lines and shapes, try looking at the grain of wood, or at slate or other rocks and minerals. Marble is an excellent source of patterns, and these can easily be painted onto the canvas ready to stitch. However, as marbling can often produce surprising designs, it is a good idea to paint the patterns on paper first, and then stitch from these using grid tracing paper. It may well be that these patterns will become the main design, rather than just a background (see Fig 3.11).

Fig 3.11 Marbling patterns on paper and canvas.

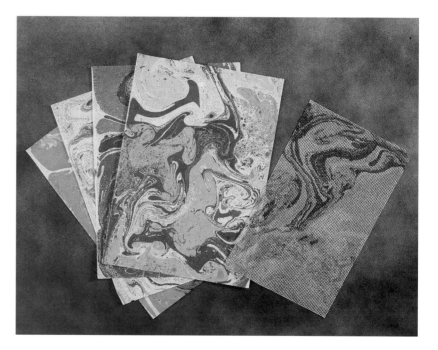

Finally, the use of decorative stitches should also be considered for adding interest to the background areas, as these are usually quicker to work than the basic stitches. The Ship project uses chequer stitch in shades of blue and green, producing a lively but not overpowering effect.

Borders

Borders have been used as a means of decoration since the very earliest times.

They have always featured strongly in needlepoint designs, providing an additional element of interest. Realistic, stylized, and abstract motifs are all suitable, but the end result tends to be more effective when linked in some way to the main design. They are usually positioned to provide a frame or edging, as in the Victorian Doll's House Carpet (Project 10). The Maple Leaf Cushion border (Project 6) is ideally placed, as it is in full view from all sides. However, it is a point to remember that where the needlepoint comes right up to the outside edges of a cushion the border is best placed a small distance in, so that it can still be easily seen. It must also be taken into consideration that in a non-square item such as the Ship Chair Seat, a straight border sewn over several rows of horizontal canvas threads may not successfully adapt to the angled chair sides. The Ship seat cover overcomes this difficulty by having a curved border with an all-over repeat pattern. There are a number of ways of dealing with the corner areas of borders, as illustrated in Fig 3.12. These examples use the whale motif from the Ship project. Butting up the horizontal line of whales in Fig 3.12a against the vertical row above or below works well with this design, but of course this does place emphasis on the horizontal stretches of border. Figure 3.12b–g all show different ways of mitring the corner. Designing a mitred corner is often aided by placing a mirror at a 45-degree angle on the border, and moving it backwards and forwards until an acceptable symmetrical solution is found. Figure 3.12b–d have the ends of the design placed against the mirror line. Unfortunately, putting the tails together leaves too large a space at the corner

Fig 3.12 Alternative corner treatments: *a* Butted, *b–g* Mitred

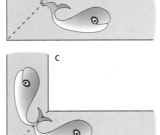

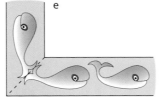

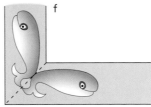

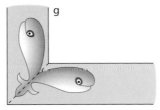

(Fig 3.12b–c), but putting the heads together works well (Fig 3.12d). However, the tails can be made to fit better by turning them downwards (Fig 3.12e–g).

Designing process examples

The three projects in this section have been based on existing commercial designs. The 'Spode Blue' Bellpull has been designed using the famous Spode Blue china as inspiration, and is based on items from ranges such as 'Geranium', 'Clifton', and 'Italian Blue'. The Ship Drop-In Seat Cover uses a tile, made by Candy Tiles, from their 'Ships' range. The Strawberry and Cherry Tray design was inspired from a wide variety of beautiful furnishing fabrics depicting fruits.

These three projects have been designed and finished not only to illustrate how effective it can be to co-ordinate stitched designs with furnishings, but also to show how easy it is to adapt an existing design that you may well have in your own home.

16 Spode Bellpull

The design of this decorative bellpull has two distinct parts: the central bouquets of flowers, and the irregularly shaped patterned border. Both have been made up of elements from several different ranges of china and, whilst contrasting sharply with each other, maintain an overall continuity by the use of one main colour of wool.

Finished size of stitching

15.5 x 46cm (6 x 18in).

How to stitch

1 Attach to a frame, mark the centre, and stitch throughout in half-cross stitch, with three strands of crewel wool.
2 Start stitching the central spray of flowers, moving on to the dark blue border outline. Once this is in position, the smaller central flowers above and below can be stitched.
3 Complete the border and its background before returning to finish the central cream background.
4 Remove from the frame and attach to the bellpull ends, referring to page 133.

For best results

The individual dark blue stitches dotted in the cream background, near the two ends, should be stitched last, into spaces which you have left for them. If these were stitched before the background, shadows of the connecting wool would be seen from the front.

Adapting the design

The two main elements of this bellpull – the floral sprays and the patterned border – can both provide further design opportunities, either together (as shown below on the cushions), or

You will need

- 14 hpi mono canvas, white, 25.5 x 56cm (10 x 22in)
- DMC Broder Medicis crewel wool:
  - 1 skein each of 8200, 8899
  - 2 skeins each of 8798, 8800
  - 4 skeins each of 8930, ecru
  - 5 skeins 8799
  - 7 skeins blanc
- tapestry needle, size 20
- lining fabric, 18.5 x 49cm (7½ x 19in)
- 2 oz (70g) polyester wadding, 15.5 x 46cm (6 x 18in)
- 2 brass bellpull ends, 16cm (6¼in) wide

individually for much smaller projects.

A full-sized repeat-patterned cushion layout is easily produced using the small floral motifs together with part of the border (see Fig 3.13). Figure 3.14 shows an alternative design, using the larger floral spray surrounded by a repeating border of honeysuckle flowers, and edged with part of the original border.

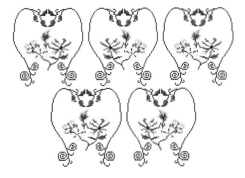

Fig 3.13 The Spode pattern adapted to an all-over repeat design.

Fig 3.14 A square design derived from the Spode pattern.

Key

8799	
8930	
8200	
8899	
8798	
8800	
ecru	
2 of blanc + 1 of ecru	

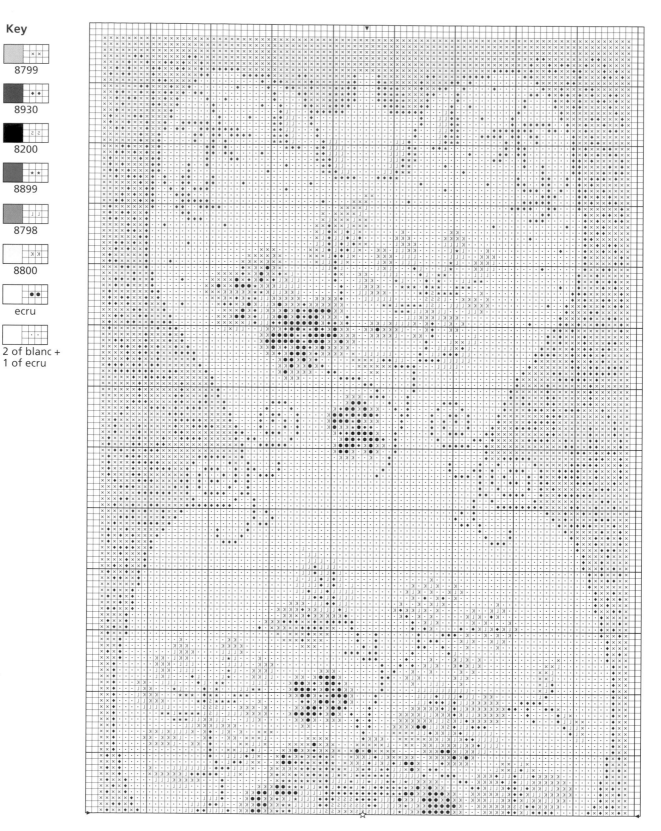

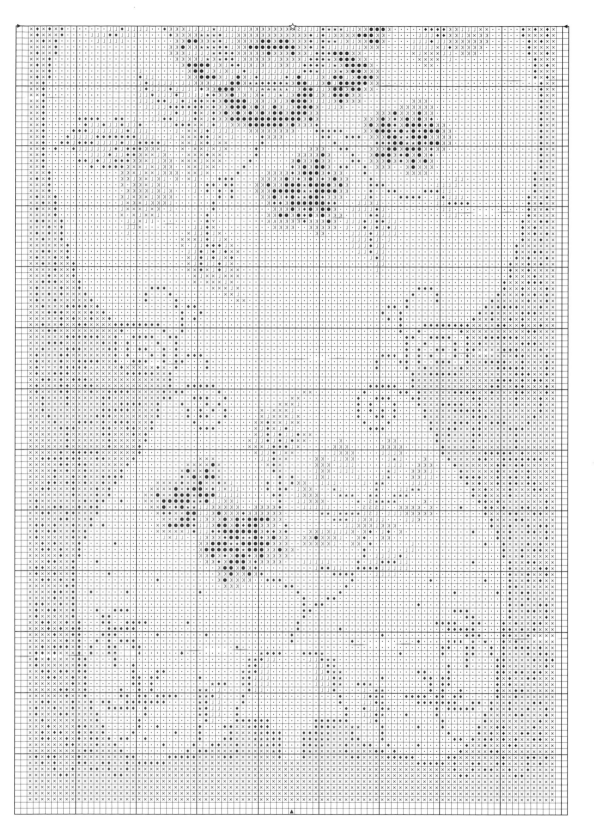

17 Ship
Drop-In
Seat Cover

This delightful small chair is a country-style Chippendale, made to a child's dimensions. The ship tile selected is one of a range of different sizes, all depicting beautiful sailing ships of a bygone age. The colours of the tapestry wool used have been kept fairly true to the tile itself, as has the actual design of the ship. This has been positioned on the flatter, central part of the chair seat, so that it can easily be seen in its entirety.

Acting as a frame around the ship is a curved border, the lines of which have been taken from the lovely curvaceous chair back. Beyond this outline is the checked border area, which extends around the edges of the seat pad. On such a project as this, it is far easier to have a wide border, avoiding straight edges which would have to be positioned an exact amount from the edges of the seat pad on all sides.

Finished size

43 x 36cm (17 x 14in)

How to stitch

1 Attach to a frame and stitch all of the ship, dark wave lines, cream sky patches, and curved border lines, in continental tent stitch.

2 The sky background and water can be stitched next, using basketweave. Beyond the frame, stitch rows of blue and green chequer stitch.

3 Remove from the frame, block or stretch if necessary, and attach to the chair seat pad, following the instructions on pages 133 and 131–2.

Adapting the design

The wide border area, with its curved edges, makes it very easy to decrease or increase the size of the finished stitched

You will need

- 11 hpi double canvas, white, 58 x 50cm (23 x 20in)
- Appletons' tapestry wool:
  - 1 skein each of 325, 326, 352, 744, 747, 873, 922, 923
  - 2 skeins 746
  - 3 skeins 742
  - 4 skeins each of 354, 927
- 1 hank each of 351, 745, 875
- tapestry needle, size 18
- 2oz (70g) polyester wadding, 43 x 36cm (17 x 14in)
- hammer and tacks
- black calico, 40 x 30cm (16 x 12in)

canvas to fit other chairs.

The whales are an element on the tile that has not been incorporated in the initial design. However, their simplified outline and shape are ideal for use as a border motif. Figure 3.15 shows a sketch of the ship with the whale border as a full-size decorative cushion. Options for the corner treatment of the border were considered on page 107.

Fig 3.15 The Ship design adapted to a square shape with the whale border.

a

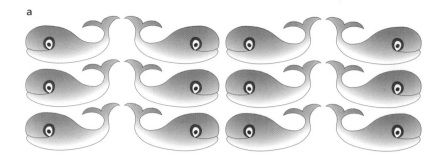

b

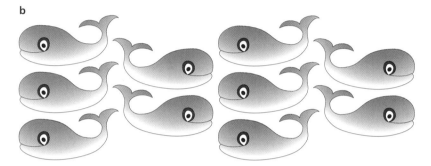

Fig 3.16 Two ways of using the whale motif as a repeat pattern.

On its own, this motif could easily be repeated to form an all-over design (see Fig 3.16a). A 'half-drop' pattern is illustrated in Fig 3.16b, whilst Fig 3.17 shows a circular arrangement. As all these are fairly simple designs, here are some suggestions to give additional interest.

- Stitch each whale in a slightly different colour – perhaps shades from green to blue and through to purple.
- Use variegated threads for either the whales or the background.
- Stitch coloured patterns on each whale – checks, stripes, spots, etc.
- Add a patterned background.

Figure 3.18 illustrates the principle of **counterchange**, where the negative background area could become the positive design area and vice versa. This area forms an interesting symmetrical shape between the whales. When mirrored downwards it makes an attractive abstract border design, bearing little resemblance to its original source (Fig 3.18b).

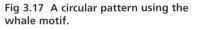

Fig 3.17 A circular pattern using the whale motif.

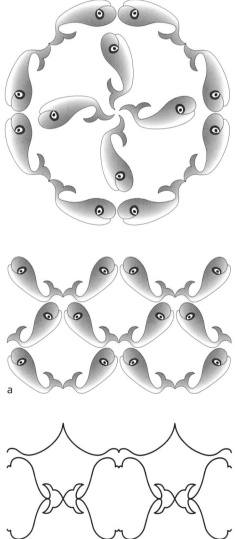

Fig 3.18 Using the negative spaces between the whale motifs.

Key

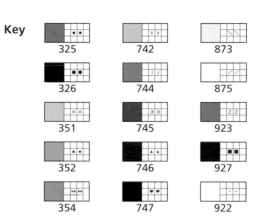

325	
326	
351	
352	
354	
742	
744	
745	
746	
747	
873	
875	
923	
927	
922	

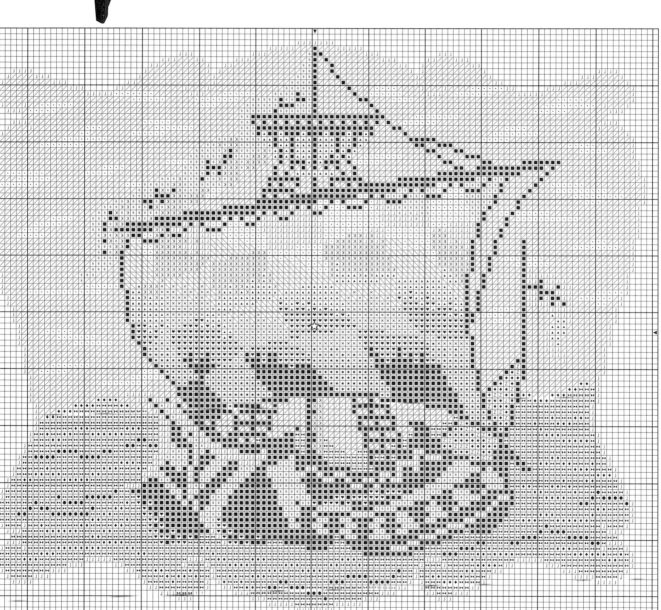

18 Strawberry
and Cherry Tray

A glance at many of the current furnishing fabrics reveal numerous fruit designs, both stylized ones and more realistic depictions of apples, pears, plums, lemons, etc. Two of my favourite summer fruits have been selected here for this simple yet effective repeat design.

The use of words and text in fabrics has also increased enormously over recent years, and has provided an attractive feature for the border to these fruits.

Finished size:

36 x 24cm (14½ x 9½in)

How to stitch

1 Attach to a frame and mark the centre of the canvas. Stitch throughout using half-cross stitch and one strand of tapestry wool.

2 Start by stitching the inside gridlines and then the inner blue borderline. The fruits within the squares can now be worked.

3 When stitching the border, work the words first, taking care to position these centrally with the gridlines.

4 Complete this project by stitching the yellow and cream backgrounds.

5 Remove from the frame and place on the tray base following the instructions on page 133.

Adapting the design

The repeat-patterned design makes it easy to increase or decrease the overall size of the project by simply adding on or removing any number of blocks of fruit, while the strawberries and cherries are ideal for using individually on small items. They are particularly suited to stitching onto waste canvas and a non-evenweave fabric, with a finer cotton thread. Items such as placemats, tablecloth, tea cosy, apron, and curtain trim would co-ordinate

You will need

- 11 hpi double or single canvas, white, 46 x 34cm (18 x 13½in)
- DMC tapestry wool:
  - 6 skeins 7745
  - 5 skeins ecru
  - 2 skeins 7033
  - 1 skein each of 7050, 7127, 7148, 7218, 7422, 7547, 7548, 7549, 7583, 7727, 7849, 7850, 7851, 7920, 7988
- tapestry needle, size 18
- a wooden tray with a flat base and glass cover measuring 36 x 24cm (14 x 9½in)

Fig 3.19 A variation on the Strawberry and Cherry design.

beautifully with the tray.

An interesting variation of this design would be to stitch all over with the strawberries and cherries without the gridlines, and then to stitch a background incorporating the writing (see Fig 3.19). This, of course, could be made to fit any size or shape – a chair or stool seat, tie-back, or whatever you like.

Key

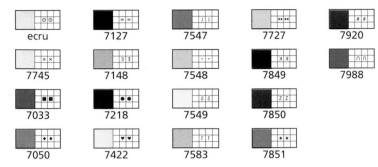

ecru | 7127 | 7547 | 7727 | 7920

7745 | 7148 | 7548 | 7849 | 7988

7033 | 7218 | 7549 | 7850

7050 | 7422 | 7583 | 7851

Computer-Assisted Design

Access to a computer is becoming more commonplace, and if one is available it can provide a useful instrument in some aspects of design. Personal computer software often includes some form of 'painting' program, some of which are quite sophisticated. These programs allow shapes to be drawn, rotated, overlaid, replicated, resized, or stretched, and sometimes allow a shape to be 'merged' into another. Combining this with 'clip-art', usually included in the same package, you can experiment with ideas and layouts, perhaps to assist in the creation of an outline pattern, or the scheme for a stencil design. If the computer has a coloured display, this can further enhance the development of ideas; however, it is unlikely that the screen will give you the colours and shades you are looking for in the finished work. Your own observation of light and shade, and colour co-ordination, will almost always surpass the capability of the computer. Printing out the design often presents a difficulty, since very few have access to printing equipment that has the colour range and accuracy required.

The advent of CD-Rom, whereby thousands of colour images may be stored on an optical disk, much like an ordinary CD, will undoubtedly change our access to valuable source material – the so-called 'electronic library of the future'. Already multi-media computers come with built-in CD-Rom players, and hundreds of disks are available covering almost every area, including art, culture, and wildlife; exploring these may prove a valuable source of inspiration.

Needlepoint design requires judgement, skill, patience, and creative flair, and both novice and expert can gain great pleasure from creating their own original work, with or without any assistance from technology.

Making-Up Instructions

This is a very exciting stage, when the project which may have taken weeks or even months to stitch will finally be finished. These step-by-step instructions will guide you through the appropriate making-up process, so that the completed article will be one you are thoroughly satisfied with.

The first task, however, is to block or stretch the canvas if it has become distorted whilst being stitched. Once the canvas is removed from the frame, it is usually very easy to see if the sides and corners are no longer square; a set square will soon confirm this. If there is only a very small amount of distortion, this may not need to be corrected if it is for an item where the stitching will be under tension and the edges firmly held in position, as in a chair seat, box lid, or stool top. If, however, the needlepoint is for a cushion or a rug, or to be laced over card, then it is important that the canvas be stretched back to 100% square.

Lightly dampen the canvas with a fine water sprayer on both sides. Mark the finished size and shape of the canvas on the blotting paper and place it with the canvas on the board, with the right side facing downwards. Pull the canvas to the correct shape onto the marked line on the blotting paper, and pin it to the board. Allow the canvas to dry thoroughly, which may take several days; the blotting paper will help to absorb the moisture. If, when the canvas is removed, it is still distorted or returns to its distorted shape after several hours, it may need re-blocking. A coat of thin wallpaper paste or iron-on Vilene is sometimes used to cover the wrong side of the corrected shape and hold it in that position. Alternatively, most needlepoint shops offer a stretching service, using a commercial stretching machine.

Blocking
You will need
- a flat wooden board
- blotting paper
- drawing pins

1 Flower Needlecase

1 Trim the canvas to within 1.5cm (⅝in) of the stitching and fold the edges to the wrong side.

2 Using a damp cloth, press this fold flat, making sure that the second row of peach stitching lies on the wrong side.

3 Mitre the corners to reduce the canvas bulk (Fig 4.1).

Fig 4.1 Mitring the corners of the canvas.

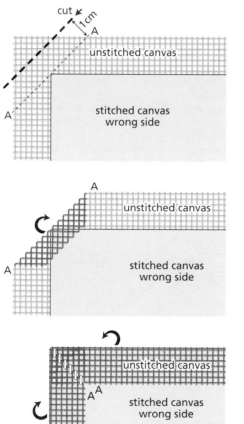

a Cut off the corner about 1cm (3/8in) from the corner of the stitched area.

b Fold the cut edge over at AA.

c Fold the sides inwards so that points AA come together to make a diagonal join, which is then stitched.

4 Slip-stitch the canvas edge to the wrong side of the needlepoint.

5 Place the wadding or interlining over the needlepoint, trimming so that it is level with the folded canvas edges.

6 Turn under the raw edges of the lining fabric and pin into place, so that all

Fig 4.2 Pinning the lining and wadding to the needlepoint.

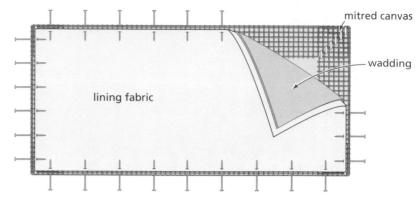

unstitched canvas is covered (Fig 4.2).

7 Slip-stitch the folded edge to hold it firmly in position.

8 Cut the felt into two pieces and edge all round using pinking shears.

9 Place these two layers of felt in the centre of the lining and attach through all the layers by neat running or back stitches in the matching doubled sewing thread (Fig 4.3).

Fig 4.3 Attaching the felt.

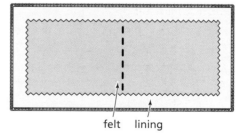

felt   lining

2 Flower and Fish Pincushion Chair Seat

The needlepoint cover is secured to the chair with upholstery tacks 10mm (⅜in) in length, for which a hammer will be needed, together with a tack remover. A few gimp pins are used to secure the ends of the braid; these are long, small-headed, coloured tacks and are available from any upholsterer. All tacks are 'temporary-tacked' first – that is, placed only half-way in, until their position is perfectly correct. This means that if any have to be repositioned they can be easily taken out using the tack remover. When all the tacks are in their final correct position they are hammered in all the way.

1 Mark the centre of each side of the chair seat, and the centre of each canvas side.

2 Place the polyester wadding over the calico on the seat, trimming the edges of the wadding so that they are level with the calico.

3 Trim away excess unstitched canvas to 2cm (¾in), then fold over to the wrong side.

4 Place this canvas on the seat, matching all the centre marks with those on the seat. Place tacks in these positions; this will ensure that the canvas goes on the chair with the warp and weft threads vertical and horizontal, even if there is a slight

amount of distortion. Pull the canvas tightly so that it is smooth and taut.

5 Continue tacking towards the corners until all the needlepoint is attached (Fig 4.4). As this is a very flat style of seat, the canvas should fit smoothly over the corners, without the need for any pleats.

6 Attach the braid by gluing, starting and finishing at the centre back of the chair, butting up together the folded ends. If necessary, make diagonal folds at the corners, and place gimp pins here, and at the central back for strength.

Making the braid

1 You will need five full skeins of Appletons' tapestry wool: two each of 622 and 703, and one of 421. Wind each of these round a small holder – cardboard tubes approximately 7–8cm (3in) long are ideal, and so are cotton reels.

2 Arrange the ends of the colours in the following order: 703 (no. 1), 622 (no. 2), 421 (no. 3), 622 (no. 4), 703 (no. 5). Knot the ends together and attach to the

central tacks in position first

Fig 4.4 Tacking the needle-point to the seat.

top of a wooden board with pins or tape. This must be secure, as the knotting of the braid will be pulling all the time. Rearrange the colours if necessary, so that they are in the correct order again.

3 Begin by picking up strand 1, wrap it over and under strand 2, forming a knot (Fig 4.5a). Holding no. 2 firmly,

pull no. 1 so that the knot is at the top.
4 Make a second knot with no. 1 in the same way.
5 It is now the turn of strand 3; wrap no. 1 over and under it, forming a knot, then repeat to form a second knot (Fig 4.5b).
6 Continue with strand 1, making knots around strands 4 and 5 in turn (Fig 4.5c).

Fig 4.5 Making the braid.

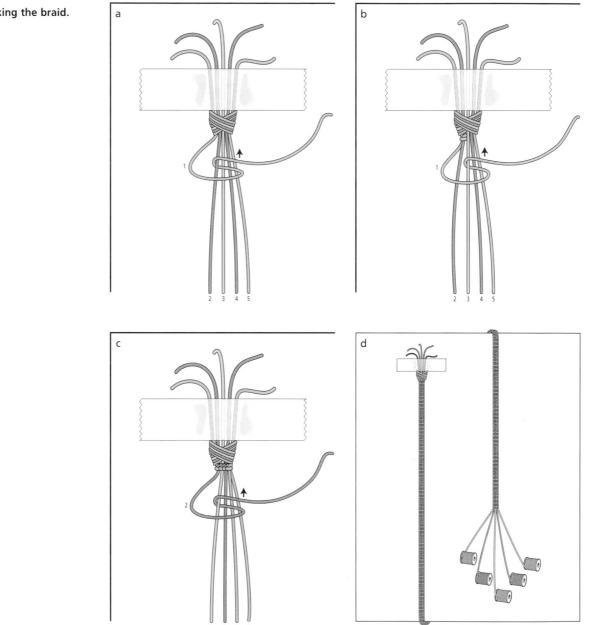

7 For the second row, start with strand 2, and make double knots over strands 3, 4, 5, and 1 in that order.

8 Continue working rows in the same way, until the braid is the correct length for the chair seat.

For best results

- At frequent intervals, the holders with the threads wound on will need to be untwisted.
- Try to pull all the knots with an even tightness, or the width of the braid will vary.
- As this is a very long length of braid to knot, when the length has reached the end of the board it should be continued over and down the other side (Fig 4.5d).

3 Carnation Repeat-Patterned Glasses Case

1 Trim the unstitched canvas edges to 2cm (¾in) on all sides, then fold the top and bottom edges to the wrong side and slip-stitch to hold them in position.

2 Place right sides together, pin, and hand or machine stitch down the two long sides.

3 Turn to the right side, gently easing out the corners.

4 Fold the cord and attach the ends to the top of the inside back edge of the case.

5 Make up the lining in the same way as the case and place inside, slip-stitching around the top edge.

6 Sew the button to the front, approximately 3cm (1¼in) from the top so that when the loop is over the button the case remains closed.

4 William Morris-Style Pincushion

1 Trim away excess canvas to within 2.5cm (1in) of the stitching.

2 Place a gathering thread approximately 1cm (½in) from the stitching, using lacing crochet cotton.

3 Place the polyester wadding over the pincushion pad and then the needlepoint on top.

4 Pull up the gathering thread and secure. Even out the gathers around the base.

5 Now lace across the back of the canvas using a large-eyed needle threaded with crochet cotton. Tie a knot at the end of the cotton and begin to lace each side to the centre. Lace from side to side in a circular motion, under and over, keeping the cotton taut (Fig 4.6). If the thread runs out, join with a reef knot. Pull each thread tightly and tie with a knot in the centre.

6 Fix to the wooden base using the given screw.

Fig 4.6 Lacing across the back of the canvas.

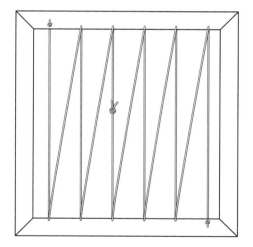

5 Rainbow Elephants Pencil Box Lid

There are two alternative methods of attaching the stitching, either by lacing or stapling. The lacing method is exactly the same as for the William Morris Pincushion (Project 4), except that pins should be placed in the calico and foam to hold the needlepoint in position, just above the wooden base edge (Fig 4.7).

Fig 4.7 Pinning the needlepoint in place before lacing.

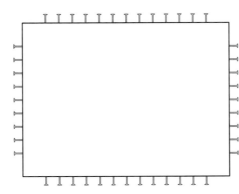

Stapling the needlepoint to the lid

1 Mark the centres of the sides of both canvas and lid.
2 Place the canvas over the polyester wadding onto the calico pad, matching up the centre marks.
3 Staple these four points approximately 1cm (½in) away from the lid edges, pulling the canvas firmly. Short staples no longer than 6mm (¼in) should be used, because of the shallow depth of the wooden base.
4 Staple from the centre towards each corner, placing the staples approximately 2cm (¾in) apart.
5 At the corners, pull the canvas down in the centre and staple. If necessary,

make two small pleats either side and staple down (Fig 4.8).
6 Trim away the excess canvas to within 1cm (½in) of the staples.
7 Attach the panel to the pencil box lid by means of the screws provided.

Fig 4.8 Stapling the corners

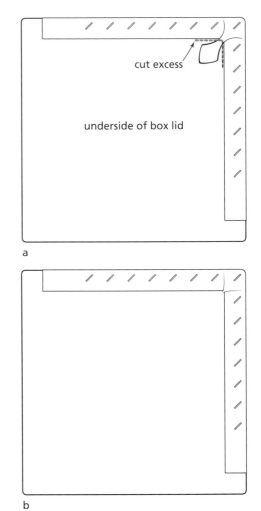

cut excess

underside of box lid

a

b

6 Maple Leaf Cushion

1 Cut the lining fabric for the back of the cushion into two pieces 43 x 23cm (17 x 9in), and the matching fabric into four triangular pieces as shown in Fig 4.9.
2 Cut the co-ordinating fabric into four

Fig 4.9 Triangular pieces for front of cushion (cut 4).

Fig 4.10 Making up the cushion front.

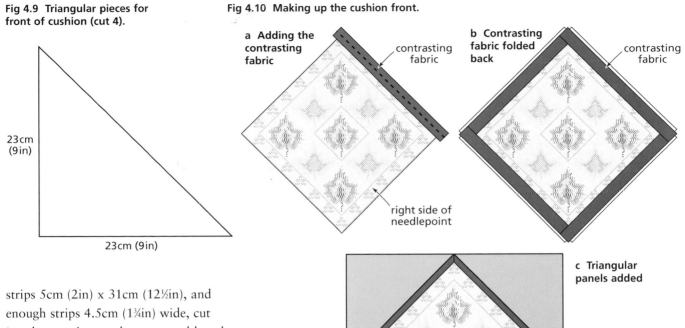

23cm (9in)

23cm (9in)

a Adding the contrasting fabric

contrasting fabric

right side of needlepoint

b Contrasting fabric folded back

contrasting fabric

c Triangular panels added

strips 5cm (2in) x 31cm (12½in), and enough strips 4.5cm (1¾in) wide, cut 'on the cross', to make up a total length of approximately 180cm (70in).

3 Place the four strips of co-ordinating fabric on the four square sides of the needlepoint, with the right sides facing. Machine stitch along the centre of each, taking care to position the stitching exactly between the last row of needle-point and the next canvas thread (Fig 4.10a). Fold the strips back against the canvas (Fig 4.10b).

4 Attach the four triangles to these strips of contrasting fabric in the same way, leaving approximately 6mm (¼in) of the contrast showing (Fig 4.10c).

5 Place together the right sides of the two pieces of fabric for the back, and machine stitch 2.5cm (1in) at each end, with a 1cm (½in) seam allowance.

6 Place the zip under the seam allowance and stitch to the fabric.

7 Make up the length of piping, joining the strips together where necessary (Fig 4.11).

8 Place this onto the right-side cushion panel, matching the raw edges, and machine stitch together. Make the join of the two ends of piping along the

bottom edge of the cushion. Join these together by trimming away any excess length of piping, leaving a seam allowance of 1.5cm (⅝in) on each side. Unpick the stitching attaching the fabric to the cord, so that the two cord ends are revealed. These are then joined by unravelling the cord ends, snipping alternate strands, intertwining them,

Fig 4.11 Joining the lengths of piping.

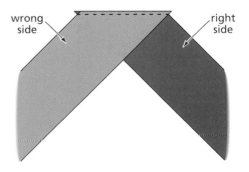

wrong side

right side

Fig 4.12 Joining the piping cord.

a Ends spliced together

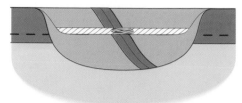

b Spliced ends bound with sewing thread

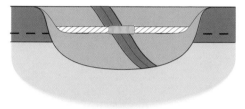

and binding with sewing thread (Fig 4.12). Refold the piping fabric over the cord and machine stitch.

9 Place the two cushion panels together, right sides facing, and machine stitch together.

10 Trim the right side and insert the cushion pad.

For best results

- When machining the piping cord casing and when attaching it to the right side, do not stitch too closely to the actual cord. When finally stitching the two sides together, this row of stitching can be close up to the cord. This will ensure that earlier rows of stitching will not show on the right side.

- Remember to open the zip before machining the two sides together, so that the cushion cover can be easily turned through to the right side.

- Small stitches will need to be made to pull the edges of the contrasting fabric together where they meet.

7 Tropical Leaf Cushion

The calico for the front of this cushion has already been sponged and stencilled (see page 49).

1 Trim the unstitched canvas to 2cm (¾in) and cut from the centre of the calico a 16.5cm (6½in) square. Clip into each corner approximately 1cm (½in) (Fig 4.13).

2 Set in the needlepoint, matching the seam allowances of 2cm (¾in). Machine through the canvas and calico, making sure that the stitching is in between the last row of needlepoint and the next canvas thread.

Fig 4.13 Cushion front prepared to receive needlepoint panel.

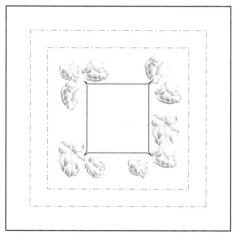

Fig 4.14 Needlepoint panel sewn in.

Fig 4.15 Turning back the border.

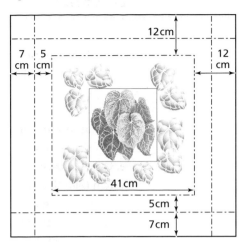

a Dimensions of border

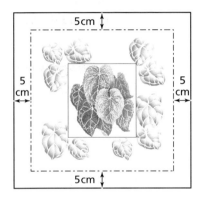

b 7cm (2¾in) turning folded to wrong side

Fig 4.16 Mitring the corners.

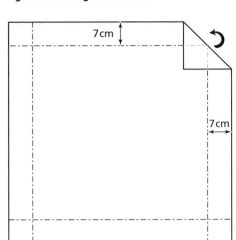

a Fold each corner over

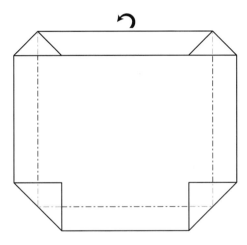

b Now fold each centre section

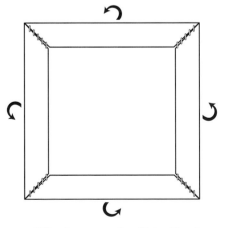

c Mitred corners slip-stitched in place

3 Using a twin needle, and the two reels of machine embroidery thread, stitch around all four sides of the needlepoint panel, approximately 0.5cm (¼in) away from the seam. This not only gives an attractive finish, but secures the seam allowances behind (Fig 4.14).

4 Fold the 7cm (2¾in) border to the wrong side (Fig 4.15).

5 At the back of the border mitre the corners as shown in Fig 4.16, slip-stitching the diagonal folds together. Now fold under the 2cm (¾in) raw edge all round.

6 Prepare the back of the cushion by inserting a zip across the centre, as for the Maple Leaf Cushion (Project 6).

7 Set in this back section under the

Fig 4.17 Tacking the back panel in place.

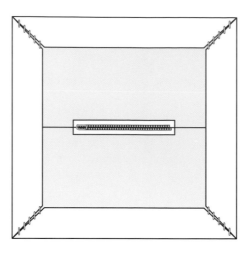

Fig 4.18 Machine stitching to produce the flanged edge.

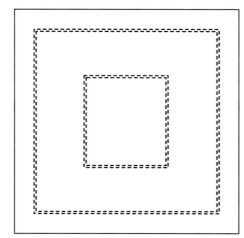

mitred border. Tack in place close to the border edge, stitching through to the cushion front (Fig 4.17).

8 Using the tacking line as a guide, machine stitch with the twin needle all the way around the border (Fig 4.18).

9 Remove the tacking stitches and insert the cushion pad.

8 Picture Frame

1 Trim the two pieces of card so that they are slightly smaller than 18 x 22cm (7 x 8¾in).

2 The piece of strong cardboard should have a 9 x 13cm (3½ x 5in) rectangle cut from the centre. The piece of polyester wadding should be cut to exactly the same size and shape.

3 Place the wadding over the strong card and then the stitched canvas on top.

4 Fold the canvas round the outside edges and pin along the top edge, securing the canvas and wadding to the card; repeat this on all sides, pulling the canvas gently. Make sure that the lines of stitching are parallel with the edges.

5 Cut the centre of the canvas into the corners and treat with Fraycheck. Pin this inner edge to the strong card as well as folding the canvas to the back.

6 Trim all the unstitched canvas to 2cm (¾in) and mitre the outer corners as for the Flower Needlecase (Project 1).

7 Lace the canvas (Fig 4.19), using the same technique as for the Pincushion (Project 4).

Fig 4.19 Lacing across the back of the Picture Frame.

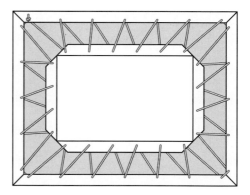

8 Dab a small amount of Fraycheck on the wrong side of the inner corners to reinforce them.

9 Place the wadding over the piece of thin card, and the backing fabric on top. Bring the edge of the backing fabric to the wrong side and glue down.

10 Place the two boards wrong sides together and slip-stitch, leaving one side open. Insert the picture or photograph, and slip-stitch the opening closed.

11 For a free-standing frame, cut a piece of thick coloured card 18 x 6cm (7 x 2¼in). Score a horizontal line approximately half-way along, and bend along this line. Attach the top half to the back of the frame with glue (Fig 4.20).

Fig 4.20 Card support for free-standing frame.

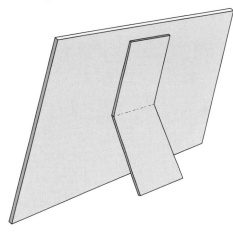

9 Rug with Decorative Panels

1 Fold the unworked canvas on all sides, so that the last row of stitching is nearly underneath. This will ensure there is no exposed canvas on the right side.

2 Trim these turnings to 4cm (1½in) and slip-stitch to the back of the canvas, using a strong linen thread and a curved needle. The corners will be flatter if they are mitred (Fig 4.21).

3 Pin a piece of hessian over the canvas, folding under the raw edges. Make sure that the hessian fold is right up to the last line of needlepoint, so that the unstitched canvas will not be visible. Slip-stitch all the way around. If you

Fig 4.21 Details of rug construction.

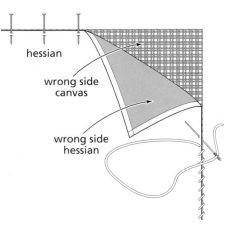

hessian

wrong side canvas

wrong side hessian

prefer the rug to be padded, then a piece of carpet felt or heavy curtain inter-lining can be laid in between the canvas and the hessian.

10 Dolls' House Carpet

1 Block the stitching if necessary, then fold under the unworked canvas on all sides, so that the last row of stitching is nearly underneath. This will ensure that there will not be any exposed canvas showing on the right side.

2 Trim these turnings to 4cm (1½in), and slip-stitch to the back of the canvas, using a strong linen thread and a curved needle. The corners will be flatter if they are mitred.

11 Georgian-Style Floral Seat Cover

This chair, because of its age, has a traditional upholstered seat pad, stuffed with horsehair rather than the more modern polyether foam. Tacks are used instead of staples, to be in keeping with the rest of the upholstery.

1 The needlepoint is placed over a piece of polyester wadding, or cotton skin wadding if preferred. The centres of the sides are matched up with centre points marked on the underside of the seat pad and temporarily tacked. More tacks are then placed along the front and back towards the corners, and down the sides. The corners are executed as for the Rainbow Elephants Pencil Box Lid (Project 5).

2 When all the tacks are hammered home and the excess trimmed away, a cover of black calico can be attached. Fold under the raw edges and tack to the underside of the seat, covering over all earlier tacks.

12 Hearts and Flowers Sewing Box Lid

This is a piece of wood covered in foam and calico, exactly the same as the Rainbow Elephants Pencil Box Lid (Project 5) but slightly larger, and is therefore attached in the same way. The staples or tacks used should be 10mm (⅜in) long. The staples should be placed at an angle, rather than parallel to the lid edge, for extra strength. This is so that the staple is lying over several canvas threads, rather than over just one or even in between threads. When making the small pleats on the corners, try to keep them as flat as possible.

13 Animal Cushion

1 Cut two pieces of fabric for the back of the cushion and insert a zip as for the Maple Leaf Cushion (Project 6), which

is the same size.

2 Fold under the raw edges of the back panel so that it measures 42cm (16½in) square, and tack it centrally to the back of the felt. Make this tacking line close and even to the fold, so that it can act as a guideline for placing the ribbon on the right side.

3 Position the ribbon over the tacking line and machine stitch close to the edge on both sides. Make a diagonal fold at each corner and hide the ends of the ribbon under one of them.

4 The edge of the felt now needs to be cut into triangles. There are nine along each side, each measuring 4cm (1½in) at the base. The amount left at each corner becomes an extra triangle, which has to be cut at a sharper angle in order to fit round the corner.

14 Needlecases in Quilting Patterns

These are made in exactly the same way as the Flower Needlecase in Project 1.

15 Space-Dyed Cushion

This is the simplest construction of the four cushions, made even more so by the back panel having a stitched opening, rather than a zip.

1 Place the front and back panels right sides together, tack, and then machine stitch as close as possible to the last line of needlepoint. Leave a 35cm (14in) opening along the bottom edge. Turn to the right side and carefully press the seam on the backing fabric, not on the needlepoint.

2 The blue shaded cord is slip-stitched to the seam line, with the ends butting up and then disappearing into the seam. The tassels on the corners are attached by stitching into the cord.

3 Insert the cushion pad and then pin and slip-stitch the side which was previously left open.

16 Spode Bellpull

1 Trim the canvas to 2cm (¾in) on all sides and then mitre the corners. Slip-stitch the lining fabric to the wrong side of the canvas.

2 After this, place over the brass rods and secure on the wrong side, again with slip-stitching.

17 Ship Drop-In Seat Cover

This chair is of a similar age to the full-sized Georgian chair (Project 11) and will have the needlepoint applied in exactly the same way.

It is a good idea to check with the older drop-in seats, such as this one, that the seat pad is still a good fit in the chair frame. Quite often the frame has loosened very slightly, leaving the seat pad looking too small. An efficient way to overcome this is to tack all round the edge of the seat pad a length of back-tacking strip, available from upholsterers. The wadding and needlepoint are then brought over this edge, covering it completely. As back-tacking strip is only available in 13mm (½in) wide cardboard, it is easy enough to cut lengths of card yourself.

18 Strawberry and Cherry Tray

1 Trim the unstitched canvas to 2.5cm (1in) on all sides, then fold to the wrong side, mitring the corners to reduce the bulk, as for the Flower Needlecase (Project 1).

2 Unscrew the wooden base and glass from the tray and place the finished stitching between them, using small dabs of glue on the four corners to hold it firmly in position. Rescrew all the layers back to the tray.

3 If preferred, lace the needlepoint over a piece of card, as for the Picture Frame (Project 8).

About
the Author

Sandra Hardy was born in Cheshire, but for many years has lived in rural Berkshire with her husband and three daughters.

As a child she spent many a happy hour trying out various crafts and different kinds of stitching. However, this was all put to one side whilst studying Social Sciences at university, and then pursuing a career in personnel management.

Her first piece of needlepoint was designed and stitched as part of an advanced City and Guilds course in Soft Furnishing, Upholstery and Design.

About this time several stitching magazines were being published, and she soon became involved in designing and stitching needlepoint projects for these. Over the years her magazine articles have diversified into blackwork, beadwork, appliqué, quilting, and cross-stitch, as well as silk painting and stencilling.

Writing and stitching for books have featured largely in recent years: Sandra has already had four books published and has contributed to two others. She combines this work with teaching adults, both locally and at national stitching exhibitions and fairs, and with running a small needlepoint kit business.

Metric
Conversion Tables

Inches to millimetres and centimetres

inches	mm	cm	inches	cm	inches	cm
⅛	3	0.3	9	22.9	30	76.2
¼	6	0.6	10	25.4	31	78.7
⅜	10	1.0	11	27.9	32	81.3
½	13	1.3	12	30.5	33	83.8
⅝	16	1.6	13	33.0	34	86.4
¾	19	1.9	14	35.6	35	88.9
⅞	22	2.2	15	38.1	36	91.4
1	25	2.5	16	40.6	37	94.0
1¼	32	3.2	17	43.2	38	96.5
1½	38	3.8	18	45.7	39	99.1
1¾	44	4.4	19	48.3	40	101.6
2	51	5.1	20	50.8	41	104.1
2½	64	6.4	21	53.3	42	106.7
3	76	7.6	22	55.9	43	109.2
3½	89	8.9	23	58.4	44	111.8
4	102	10.2	24	61.0	45	114.3
4½	114	11.4	25	63.5	46	116.8
5	127	12.7	26	66.0	47	119.4
6	152	15.2	27	68.6	48	121.9
7	178	17.8	28	71.1	49	124.5
8	203	20.3	29	73.7	50	127.0

Metric and Imperial Canvases

Holes per 10cm	Holes per inch
26	6/7
30	7/8
34	8/9
38	9/10
40	10
42	10/11
44	11
46	11/12
48	12
52	13
56	14
60	15
70	18
80	20

Index

A

Animal Cushion 81–4, 132
Anthurium magnificum columbia 47
Appletons' crewel wool 2, 45

B

backgrounds 106
Bargello stitch 10, 34
basketweave stitch 20–4, Fig 1.7
    Carnation Glasses Case 22–4
    method 20
beadwork 74–8
    Hearts and Flowers Sewing Box
        Lid 76–8
    method 75
Beeton, Mrs: *Book of Needlework* 68
Bellpull 108–11, 133
Berlin wools 44, 63
Bess of Hardwick 25
Blair Castle 63
blocking 1, 121
blue line canvas *see* waste canvas
borders 17, 106–7, 113
braid 123–5
brick stitch 35, Fig 1.16a
    Maple Leaf Cushion Panel 37–41
Byzantine stitch 55, Fig.2.6, 56

C

canvas
    beadwork 74–5
    crewel wool shading 45
    decorative stitches 52–3
    design and 103
    distortion of 4–5
    experimentation 98
    joining 60–2
    mesh size 2
    petit point 64
    preparation for stitching 6
    tramming 69
    transferring design onto 105–6
    types of 1–2
    waste canvas 79
Carnation Repeat-Patterned Glasses
    Case 22–4, 125
chair seat covers *see* seat covers
charts 7
chequer stitch 58, 59, Fig 2.8a, Fig 2.8e
cleaning needlepoint 7

colour
    design 103–5
    experimenting with 88–98
colour wheel 103–4
complementary colours 103–4
computer-assisted design 119
continental tent stitch 4, 10–19, 64
    Flower and Fish Chair Seat 15–19
    Flower Needlecase 13–14
    methods 10–12, Figs 1.1–1.5
cotton yarns 3, 64
counterchange 114
crewel wool 2–3, 64
crewel wool shading 44–50
    method 45
    Tropical Leaf Cushion 46–50
cross stitch 10, 25–33, 60
    methods 26, 53
    oblong cross stitch 58, 59, Fig 2.8c
    Rainbow Elephants Pencil Box Lid
        31–3
    upright cross stitch 58, 59, Fig 2.8d
    varieties 25
    William Morris-Style Pincushion
        28–30
cushion stitch 55, Fig 2.6c
cushions
    Animal Cushion 82–5, 132
    Maple Leaf Panel 37–41, 126–8
    Space-Dyed Cushion 94–6, 132–3
    Tropical Leaf Panel 46–50, 128–30

D

decorative stitches 51–62
    methods 53
    Picture Frame 54–6
    Rug with Decorative Panels 57–62
design 99–119
    backgrounds 106
    borders 106–7
    computer-assisted 119
    Ship Drop-In Seat Cover 112–15
    Spode Bellpull 108–11
    steps 99–106
    Strawberry and Cherry Tray 116–18
diagonal tent stitch *see* basketweave
    stitch
DMC Broder Medicis wool 2, 32, 45
Dolls' House Carpet 65–7, 131
double canvas 1, 63, 64, 69
double straight cross stitch 25, Fig 1.8c

E

Elephants Pencil Box Lid 31–3, 126
embroidery hoop 5
exploded picture 100

F

fabric paints 97–8, 105
Fassett, Kaffe 35
finder/viewer 100
finishing off 7
Floral Seat Cover 70–3, 131–2
Florentine stitch 10, 34, 51, 52, 55,
    Fig 2.6b, 56
    old Florentine stitch 35, Fig 1.16c
Flower and Fish Pincushion Chair
    Seat 15–19, 122–5
Flower Needlecase 13–14, 122
frames 4–5

G

Georgian-Style Floral Seat Cover
    70–3, 131–2
gimp pins 122–3
Glamis Castle 63
glasses case 22–4, 125
Gobelin stitch 51
    upright Gobelin stitch 34, 36
graph paper 105–6
gros point 63, 64

H

half-cross stitch 25, 27, Fig 1.12, 64
    method 30
half-cushion stitch 55, Fig 2.6, 56
harmonious colours 103–4
Hearts and Flowers Sewing Box Lid
    76–8, 132
Hungarian diamond 35, Fig 1.16d
Hungarian point stitch 34
Hungarian stitch 35, Fig 1.16b

I

interlock canvas 1, 69
Irish stitch 34
Italian three-sided cross stitch 25, Fig 1.8a

L

lacing 125, 126

Leviathan stitch 52, Fig 2.5c

M

making-up instructions 121–33
Maple Leaf Cushion 37–41, 126–8
marbling 106
Mary, Queen of Scots 25, 63
metric conversion tables 135
mille-point 63
mistakes 7
mitring corners 107, 122
mono canvas 1, 69
Montenegrin cross stitch 25, Fig 1.8b
motifs: designing 101–2

N

needlecases
    Flower 13–14, 122
    Quilting Patterns 88–92, 132
needles 3, 45, 53
    beadwork 75
    petit point 64
    threading 3–4
    tramming 69
    waste canvas 80

O

oblong cross stitch 58, 59, Fig 2.8c
old Florentine stitch 35, Fig 1.16c
Owen, Mrs Henry: *The Illuminated Book of Needlework* 20
Oxburgh hangings 25

P

paints, fabric 97–8, 105
palettes (thread organizers) 6
paper-shape motifs 101
Parisian stitch 35, 36, Fig 1.16e
Paterna yarn 2, 44, 45
Pencil Box Lid 31–3, 126
Penelope (double) canvas 1, 63, 64, 69
Persian wool 2–3
petit point 63–7
    method 64
    Victorian Dolls' House Carpet 65–7
Picture Frame 54–6, 130–1
Pincushion 28–30, 125
Pincushion Seat Cover 15–19, 122–5
piping cord 127–9
plastic canvas 1
plush stitch 51, Fig 2.5b
point d'Hongrie 34

Q

quilting designs 88–92, 132

R

Rainbow Elephants Pencil Box Lid 31–3, 126
random straight stitch 35
repairs 7
repeating patterns 101, 114, 117
    Glasses Case 22–4, 125
Rhodes stitch 52, Fig 2.5d, 56
rococo stitch 51, Fig 2.5a
rotating frame 4
rug wool 3
rugs 53
    Rug with Decorative Panels 57–62, 131
    Victorian Dolls' House Carpet 65–7, 131

S

satin stitch 55, Fig 2.6a, 56
Scotch stitch 58, 59, Fig 2.8b
seat covers
    Flower and Fish 15–19, 122–5
    Georgian-Style Floral 70–3, 131–2
    Ship Drop-In Cover 112–15, 133
Sewing Box Lid 76–8, 132
Ship Drop-In Seat Cover 112–15, 133
single (mono) canvas 1, 69
slate frames 4
slips 63
space dyeing 93–6
    method 93
    Space-Dyed Cushion 94–6, 132–3
Spode Bellpull 108–11, 133
sponging 49
stab stitch method 80
Standon House 63–4
stapling 126
starting to stitch 7
stencilling 32, 48, 49
stitches
    crewel wool shading 45
    decorative stitches 53
    design and 103
    waste canvas 80
    see also under individual types
straight stitch 34–41
    Maple Leaf Cushion Panel 37–41
    method 36
    varieties 34–6
stranded cottons 3, 64
Strawberry and Cherry Tray 116–18, 133
stretcher frame 4

T

tacking 122–3
tapestry wool 2–3
tear-away canvas *see* waste canvas

tent stitch 25
    continental *see* continental tent stitch
    diagonal *see* basketweave stitch
texture: experimentation with 88–98
thread organizers 6
threads/yarns
    beadwork 74, 75
    crewel wool shading 45
    decorative stitches 53
    design 102–3
    estimation of quantity 105
    experimentation with colour and texture 88–98
    petit point 64
    tramming 69
    types of 2–3
    waste canvas 79
    see also under individual types
tie-dyeing 97
tramming 68–73, Fig 2.10, 77
    Georgian-Style Seat Cover 70–3
    method 69
Tray 116–18, 133
Tropical Leaf Cushion 46–50, 128–30
tubular PVC frames 4–5

U

upright cross stitch 58, 59, Fig 2.8d
upright Gobelin stitch 34, 36

V

Victorian Dolls' House Carpet 65–7, 131
viewer/finder 100

W

waste canvas 1, 79–85
    Animal Cushion 82–5
    method 80
William Morris-Style Pincushion 28–30, 125
wools 2–3

Y

yarns *see* threads/yarns

TITLES AVAILABLE FROM
GMC Publications

BOOKS

WOODWORKING

40 More Woodworking Plans & Projects . . . . *GMC Publications*
Bird Boxes and Feeders for the Garden . . . . *Dave Mackenzie*
Complete Woodfinishing . . . . *Ian Hosker*
Electric Woodwork . . . . *Jeremy Broun*
Furniture & Cabinetmaking Projects . . . . *GMC Publications*
Furniture Projects . . . . *Rod Wales*
Furniture Restoration (Practical Crafts) . . . . *Kevin Jan Bonner*
Furniture Restoration and Repair for Beginners . . . . . . *Kevin Jan Bonner*
Green Woodwork . . . . *Mike Abbott*
The Incredible Router . . . . *Jeremy Broun*
Making & Modifying Woodworking Tools . . . . *Jim Kingshott*
Making Chairs and Tables . . . . *GMC Publications*
Making Fine Furniture . . . . *Tom Darby*
Making Little Boxes from Wood . . . . *John Bennett*
Making Shaker Furniture . . . . *Barry Jackson*
Pine Furniture Projects for the Home . . . . *Dave Mackenzie*
Sharpening Pocket Reference Book . . . . *Jim Kingshott*
Sharpening: The Complete Guide . . . . *Jim Kingshott*
Stickmaking: A Complete Course . . . . *Andrew Jones & Clive George*
Woodfinishing Handbook (Practical Crafts) . . . . *Ian Hosker*
Woodworking Plans and Projects . . . . *GMC Publications*
The Workshop . . . . *Jim Kingshott*

WOODTURNING

Adventures in Woodturning . . . . *David Springett*
Bert Marsh: Woodturner . . . . *Bert Marsh*
Bill Jones' Notes from the Turning Shop . . . . *Bill Jones*
Bill Jones' Further Notes from the Turning Shop . . . . *Bill Jones*
Colouring Techniques for Woodturners . . . . *Jan Sanders*
Decorative Techniques for Woodturners . . . . *Hilary Bowen*
Essential Tips for Woodturners . . . . *GMC Publications*
Faceplate Turning . . . . *GMC Publications*
Fun at the Lathe . . . . *R.C. Bell*
Illustrated Woodturning Techniques . . . . *John Hunnex*
Intermediate Woodturning Projects . . . . *GMC Publications*
Keith Rowley's Woodturning Projects . . . . *Keith Rowley*
Make Money from Woodturning . . . . *Ann & Bob Phillips*
Multi-Centre Woodturning . . . . *Ray Hopper*
Pleasure and Profit from Woodturning . . . . *Reg Sherwin*
Practical Tips for Turners & Carvers . . . . *GMC Publications*
Practical Tips for Woodturners . . . . *GMC Publications*
Spindle Turning . . . . *GMC Publications*
Turning Miniatures in Wood . . . . *John Sainsbury*
Turning Wooden Toys . . . . *Terry Lawrence*

Understanding Woodturning . . . . *Ann & Bob Phillips*
Useful Techniques for Woodturners . . . . *GMC Publications*
Useful Woodturning Projects . . . . *GMC Publications*
Woodturning: A Foundation Course . . . . *Keith Rowley*
Woodturning: A Source Book of Shapes . . . . *John Hunnex*
Woodturning Jewellery . . . . *Hilary Bowen*
Woodturning Masterclass . . . . *Tony Boase*
Woodturning Techniques . . . . *GMC Publications*
Woodturning Test Reports . . . . *GMC Publications*
Woodturning Wizardry . . . . *David Springett*

WOODCARVING

The Art of the Woodcarver . . . . *GMC Publications*
Carving Birds & Beasts . . . . *GMC Publications*
Carving on Turning . . . . *Chris Pye*
Carving Realistic Birds . . . . *David Tippey*
Decorative Woodcarving . . . . *Jeremy Williams*
Essential Tips for Woodcarvers . . . . *GMC Publications*
Essential Woodcarving Techniques . . . . *Dick Onians*
Lettercarving in Wood: A Practical Course . . . . *Chris Pye*
Practical Tips for Turners & Carvers . . . . *GMC Publications*
Understanding Woodcarving . . . . *GMC Publications*
Useful Techniques for Woodcarvers . . . . *GMC Publications*
Wildfowl Carving - Volume 1 . . . . *Jim Pearce*
Wildfowl Carving - Volume 2 . . . . *Jim Pearce*
The Woodcarvers . . . . *GMC Publications*
Woodcarving: A Complete Course . . . . *Ron Butterfield*
Woodcarving: A Foundation Course . . . . *Zoë Gertner*
Woodcarving for Beginners . . . . *GMC Publications*
Woodcarving Test Reports . . . . *GMC Publications*
Woodcarving Tools, Materials & Equipment . . . . *Chris Pye*

UPHOLSTERY

Seat Weaving (Practical Crafts) . . . . *Ricky Holdstock*
Upholsterer's Pocket Reference Book . . . . *David James*
Upholstery: A Complete Course . . . . *David James*
Upholstery Restoration . . . . *David James*
Upholstery Techniques & Projects . . . . *David James*

TOYMAKING

Designing & Making Wooden Toys . . . . *Terry Kelly*
Fun to Make Wooden Toys & Games . . . . *Jeff & Jennie Loader*
Making Board, Peg & Dice Games . . . . *Jeff & Jennie Loader*
Making Wooden Toys & Games . . . . *Jeff & Jennie Loader*
Restoring Rocking Horses . . . . *Clive Green & Anthony Dew*

DOLLS' HOUSES

Architecture for Dolls' Houses . . . . *Joyce Percival*
Beginners' Guide to the Dolls' House Hobby . . . . *Jean Nisbett*
The Complete Dolls' House Book . . . . *Jean Nisbett*
Dolls' House Bathrooms: Lots of Little Loos . . . . *Patricia King*
Easy to Make Dolls' House Accessories . . . . *Andrea Barham*
Make Your Own Dolls' House Furniture . . . . *Maurice Harper*
Making Dolls' House Furniture . . . . *Patricia King*
Making Georgian Dolls' Houses . . . . *Derek Rowbottom*
Making Miniature Oriental Rugs & Carpets . . . . . *Meik & Ian McNaughton*
Making Period Dolls' House Accessories . . . . *Andrea Barham*
Making Period Dolls' House Furniture . . . . . *Derek & Sheila Rowbottom*
Making Tudor Dolls' Houses . . . . *Derek Rowbottom*
Making Unusual Miniatures . . . . *Graham Spalding*
Making Victorian Dolls' House Furniture . . . . *Patricia King*
Miniature Needlepoint Carpets . . . . *Janet Granger*
The Secrets of the Dolls' House Makers . . . . *Jean Nisbett*

THE HOME

Home Ownership: Buying and Maintaining . . . . *Nicholas Snelling*

CRAFTS

Celtic Knotwork Designs . . . . *Sheila Sturrock*
Collage from Seeds, Leaves and Flowers . . . . *Joan Carver*
Complete Pyrography . . . . *Stephen Poole*
Creating Knitwear Designs . . . . *Pat Ashforth & Steve Plummer*
Cross Stitch Kitchen Projects . . . . *Janet Granger*
Cross Stitch on Colour . . . . *Sheena Rogers*
Embroidery Tips & Hints . . . . *Harold Hayes*
An Introduction to Crewel Embroidery . . . . *Mave Glenny*
Making Character Bears . . . . *Valerie Tyler*
Making Greetings Cards for Beginners . . . . *Pat Sutherland*
Making Knitwear Fit . . . . *Pat Ashforth & Steve Plummer*
Needlepoint: A Foundation Course . . . . *Sandra Hardy*
Pyrography Handbook (Practical Crafts) . . . . *Stephen Poole*
Tassel Making for Beginners . . . . *Enid Taylor*
Tatting Collage . . . . *Lindsay Rogers*
Temari: A Traditional Japanese Embroidery Technique . . . . *Margaret Ludlow*

Security for the Householder: Fitting Locks and Other Devices . . . *E. Phillips*

VIDEOS

Drop-in and Pinstuffed Seats . . . . *David James*
Stuffover Upholstery . . . . *David James*
Elliptical Turning . . . . *David Springett*
Woodturning Wizardry . . . . *David Springett*
Turning Between Centres: The Basics . . . . *Dennis White*
Turning Bowls . . . . *Dennis White*
Boxes, Goblets and Screw Threads . . . . *Dennis White*
Novelties and Projects . . . . *Dennis White*
Classic Profiles . . . . *Dennis White*
Twists and Advanced Turning . . . . *Dennis White*
Sharpening the Professional Way . . . . *Jim Kingshott*
Sharpening Turning & Carving Tools . . . . *Jim Kingshott*
Bowl Turning . . . . *John Jordan*
Hollow Turning . . . . *John Jordan*
Woodturning: A Foundation Course . . . . *Keith Rowley*
Carving a Figure: The Female Form . . . . *Ray Gonzalez*
The Router: A Beginner's Guide . . . . *Alan Goodsell*
The Scroll Saw: A Beginner's Guide . . . . *John Burke*

MAGAZINES

WOODTURNING • WOODCARVING • THE DOLLS' HOUSE MAGAZINE • FURNITURE & CABINETMAKING

BUSINESSMATTERS • CREATIVE IDEAS FOR THE HOME • THE ROUTER

•

The above represents a full list of all titles currently published or scheduled to be published. All are available direct from the Publishers or through bookshops, newsagents and specialist retailers. To place an order, or to obtain a complete catalogue, contact:

GMC Publications,
166 High Street, Lewes, East Sussex BN7 1XU, United Kingdom
Tel: 01273 488005 Fax: 01273 478606

Orders by credit card are accepted